Coping with Stress in Teaching

Stress in Modern Society: No. 3

Other Titles in This Series:

STRESS IN
MODERN SOCIETY
Number 3

Coping with Stress in Teaching

Joy N. Humphrey
James H. Humphrey

AMS PRESS, INC.
New York

Library of Congress Cataloging-in-Publication Data

Humphrey, Joy N.
  Coping with stress in teaching.

  (Stress in modern society ; no. 3)
  Includes index.
  1. Teachers—Job stress. 2. Teachers—Job stress—
Prevention. 3. Stress (Psychology)—Prevention.
I. Humphrey, James Harry, 1911-   . II. Title.
III. Series.
LB2840.2.H86 1986   371.1'001'9   86-14195
ISBN 0-404-63253-X

Published by
AMS Press, Inc.
56 East 13th Street
New York, N.Y. 10003

MANUFACTURED IN THE UNITED STATES OF AMERICA

CONTENTS

COPING WITH STRESS IN TEACHING

Joy N. Humphrey, M.S.
and
James H. Humphrey, Ed.D

About the Authors

Although father-daughter writing teams are not un-known, they are rather rare. Joy N. Humphrey, a former elementary school classroom teacher and stress management consultant received her graduate degree from Johns Hopkins University. A stress education specialist, she is the co-author of four books and several articles in professional journals. In addition, she contributed two chapters to *Stress in Childhood*, the first book in this series.

James H. Humphrey, Professor Emeritus at the University of Maryland is the Editor of the AMS series on Stress in Modern Society. He is the author or coauthor of over 40 books and 200 articles and research reports.

The authors collaborated on certain aspects of stress research with the late Hans Selye who was often referred to as the father of Stress.

INTRODUCTION

In recent years a voluminous literature has appeared in both the scientific community and in popular sources in the area of stress. Very little of this has been directed specifically to teachers. Thus, the express purpose of this book is to provide materials on stress pertinent to teachers and teaching conditions and situations.

An examination of the title of the book, *Coping with Stress in Teaching* may be in order. In the first place, "how to" self-help books have become so numerous that in the eyes of some readers they may tend to lack credibility. This is valid, of course, if a reader expects definitive answers to the solution of problems. On the other hand, if such a book is viewed as a *guide* rather than a *recipe*, it is likely that more value will be derived from it. In the case of the present book just such an attitude should prevail as one reads it.

Although numerous suggestions and recommendations are made for coping with stress, the reader must take into account those individual differences that prevail in all of us. In other words, what works for one person may not work for another. In this regard, the word *coping* itself means "dealing with and attempting to overcome problems."

It should be understood that underlying conditions causing such problems differ, individuals dealing with the problems differ, and procedures for dealing with the problems differ.

Although this book is concerned with stress in teaching, this does not mean that stress resulting from other life events should be overlooked. Certainly, teachers as well as others are subjected to stress in situations not related to the job. However, the main focus of this book is to take into account those stressful conditions that are relevant to the profession of teaching. To this end the intent is to familiarize the reader with some of the basic facets and ramifications concerned with stress, as well as to consider possible actions that might be taken in dealing with it.

It is possible that the suggestions made throughout the book can meet with varying degrees of success with persons who practice them. However, of utmost importance is the fact that a positive attitude toward life in general is an essential prerequisite for any kind of stress management program that is undertaken.

CHAPTER 1

THE MEANING OF STRESS

An intelligent discussion of any subject should perhaps begin with some sort of understanding about the terminology employed or, in other words, the language and vocabulary used to communicate about a given subject. There are several important reasons why a book on stress, in particular, should begin by establishing such a general frame of reference. For one thing, our review of several hundred pieces of literature concerned with stress has revealed that the terminology connected with it is voluminous, sometimes contradictory and, to say the least, rather confusing. Many times, terms with different meanings are likely to be used interchangeably; conversely, the same term may be used under various circumstances to denote several different meanings. That this results in confusion for the reader is obvious, because such usage of terminology is likely to generate a situation of multiple meanings in the general area of stress. In this regard, our interviews and surveys of large numbers of teachers have revealed a wide variety of understandings with reference to the meaning of stress.

It should be understood at the outset that we are not attempting to develop a set of standardized stress-related terms. This would be well-nigh impossible. The purpose is for communication only, and limited to the aims of this particular book. This is to say that if a term is used in the book you will know what we mean by it. We will try to develop working descriptions of terms for the purpose of communicating with you, the reader. In no sense are we trying to impose a terminology upon you. If you prefer other terms you should feel free to use them in your communication with others.

For the discussion of terminology that follows, we will resort in some instances to terms used by various authorities in the field, and in others, insofar as they may be available, to

1

pure technical definitions. It should be understood that many of the terms that we will allude to have some sort of general meaning attached to them. An attempt will be made in some cases to start with this general meaning and give it specificity for the subject at hand.

STRESS

There is no solid agreement regarding the derivation of the term stress. For example, one source suggests that the term is derived from the Latin word *stringere*, meaning "to bind tightly." (38). A second source contends that the term derives from the French word *destresse* (Anglicized to *distress*) and suggests that the prefix "dis-" was eventually eliminated because of slurring, as in the case of the word "because" becoming "cause." (71).

A common generalized literal description of the term stress is a "constraining force or influence." When applied to the human organism this could be interpreted to mean the extent to which the body can withstand a given force or influence. In this regard, one of the most often quoted descriptions of stress is that of the famous pioneer in the field, Dr. Hans Selye, who described it as the "nonspecific response of the body to any demand." (71) This means that stress involves a mobilization of the bodily resources in response to some sort of stimulus. These responses can include various physical and chemical changes in the organism. This description of stress could be extended by saying that it involves demands that tax and/or exceed the resources of the human organism. This means that stress not only involves these bodily responses, but that it also involves wear and tear on the organism brought about by these responses. In essence, stress can be considered as any factor acting internally or externally that makes it difficult to adapt and that demands increased effort from the person to maintain a state of equilibrium within himself and with his external environment. It should be understood that stress is a state that one is in, and this should not be confused with any agent that produces such a state. These are called *stressors* and they will be discussed in various ways throughout the book.

TENSION

Since the term *tension* is frequently used in relation to stress, we should consider the meaning of this term. It is interesting in this connection to note the entries used for *stress* and *tension* in the *Education Index*. This bibliographical index of periodical educational literature records entries on these two terms as follows:

Stress (physiology)
Stress (psychology): See *Tension* (psychology)
Tension (physiology): See *Stress* (physiology)
Tension (psychology)

This indicates that there are physiological and psychological aspects to both stress and tension. However, the way in which stress articles are classified seems to imply that stress is something more physiological, and that tension is more psychological. Thus, the terms *psychological stress* and *psychological tension* could be interpreted as meaning the same thing. The breakdown in this position is seen where there is another entry for tension concerned with *muscular* tension. The latter, of course, must be considered to have a physiological orientation. In the final analysis, the validity of these entries will depend upon the point of view of each individual. As we shall see later the validity of this particular classification may be at odds with a more specific meaning of these terms.

The late Dr. Arthur Steinhaus, a notable physiologist, considered tensions as any unnecessary or exaggerated muscle contractions, which could be accomplished by abnormally great or reduced activities of the internal organs.

(75) He viewed tensions in two frames of reference; first, as *physiologic* or *unlearned tensions*, and second, as *psychologic* or *learned tensions*. An example of the first, physiologic or unlearned tensions, would be "tensing" at bright lights or intense sounds. He regarded psychologic, or learned tensions as responses to stimuli that ordinarily do not involve muscular contractions, but that at some earlier time were associated with a situation in which tension was a part of the normal response. In view of the fact that the brain connects any events that stimulate it simultaneously, it would appear to follow that, depending upon the unlimited kinds of personal experiences one might have, he may show tension to any and all kinds of stimuli. An example of psychologic or learned tension would be an inability to relax when riding in a car after experiencing or imagining too many automobile accidents.

In a sense, it may be inferred that physiologic or unlearned tensions are current and spontaneous, while psychologic or learned tensions may be latent as a result of a previous experience and may emerge at a later time. Although there may be a hairline distinction, perhaps the essential difference between stress and tension is that the former involves a physical and/or mental state concerned with wear and tear on the organism, while the latter is either a spontaneous or latent condition which can bring about this wear and tear.

EMOTION

In view of the fact that the terms stress and emotion are used interchangeably in the literature, consideration should be given to the meaning of the latter term. A good description of the term *emotion* is one given by Drs. Frieda and Ralph Merry, who view it as the response an individual makes when confronted with a situation for which he is unprepared or which he interprets as a possible source of gain or loss for him. (50) For example, if an individual is confronted with a situation for which he may not have a satisfactory response, the emotional pattern of fear could result. Of, if he finds himself in a position where his desires are frustrated, the emotional pattern of anger may occur. Emotion, then, is not the state of stress itself but rather it is a stressor that can stimulate stress.

ANXIETY

Another term often used to mean the same thing as stress is *anxiety*. In fact, some of the literature uses the expression "anxiety *or* stress," implying that they are one and the same thing. A basic literal meaning of the term anxiety is "uneasiness of the mind," but this simple generalization may be more complex than it looks at first sight. For example, Dr. C. Eugene Walker points up the fact that psychologists who deal with this area in detail have difficulty defining the term. He gives his own description of it as the reaction to a situation where we believe our well-being is endangered or threatened in some way. (80) Dr. David Viscott considers anxiety as the fear of hurt or loss. He contends that this leads to anger with anger leading to guilt, and guilt, unrelieved, leading to depression. (79)

Anxiety should not necessarily be considered identical to stress. Rather it can be thought of as a combination of certain emotional patterns, principally anger and fear, that can place one in a condition that can bring about stress.

PSYCHOSOMATIC

A final term that we will take into account at this point is *psychosomatic*. The literal meaning of the term is *mind and body (psyche,* meaning mind and *soma,* meaning body). A relatively new discipline called *psychophysiology* is concerned with intricate, complex and interfused relationships between mind and body, (10) and any theory of stress must be concerned with this basic concept.

TEACHERS' CONCEPTS OF STRESS

In view of the fact that the term stress appears to mean so many different things to different people, we considered it appropriate to try to get some idea of teachers' concepts of it. This was accomplished by having several hundred teachers fill in the sentence completion item, Stress is _____. The following discussion is based upon the data derived from this source.

One would expect a rather wide variety of responses from teachers regarding their concepts of stress, particularly since "experts" themselves are not in complete agreement on this question. Our consideration of teachers' concepts of stress focused on the number of times certain *key* words emerged in the responses. By identifying such key words we felt that we could make a fairly valid assessment of how teachers conceived of what stress means to them.

The word *pressure* appeared in 44 percent of the responses. This was by far the most popular key word, and by almost a two-to-one margin over all other key words combined. This is interesting, because the word pressure rarely appears in the literature on stress except when it is used in connection with *blood pressure.* It is also interesting to note that the lead definition of the term in most standard dictionaries considers it in relation to the human organism by referring to pressure as "burden of physical or mental distress."

Some representative examples of how teachers used the word pressure in describing their concept of stress follow:
Stress is:
emotional pressure.
physical and psychological consequences of internal and external pressure.

working under undue pressure.
pressure caused by sources known and unknown.
a feeling of being unable to cope with pressure.
pressure harmful to health.

The key word appearing the next most frequently, at 15 percent of the time, was *tension.* In our discussion of tension above, where we considered physiologic or unlearned tensions as well as psychologic or learned tensions, we made an arbitrary differentiation between stress and tension, according to which the essential difference is that the former is a physical and/or mental state involving wear and tear on the organism, while the latter is either a spontaneous or latent condition that can bring about this wear and tear.

Most often those teachers who used the term tension in connection with their concept of stress did so in the following manner:

Stress is:
a feeling of tension.
those factors that cause tension.
tension that is harmful to health.
tension that occurs as a result of pressure.

Following closely behind the word tension was the key word *frustration* used by 13 percent of the teachers in describing their concept of stress. We consider frustration to be a result of one's needs (basic demands) not being met. Thus, stress can be induced as a result of frustration. This means that frustration is not the same as stress but that it becomes a stressor when one is frustrated because one's needs are not being met. In any event many of those teachers who conceived frustration as stress used the term as follows:

Stress is:
frustration from complying with orders.
frustration in the environment that influences performance.
frustration that results in a mental or emotional state that disrupts routine.

frustration causing inner conflict.
frustration that consumes daily mental activity.
frustration caused by having to do something you
  don't want to do.

In ten percent of the responses the key word used to express the concept of stress was *strain*. Like the term pressure, the word strain is used very little in the literature on stress. It may be recalled that some derive the term stress from the Latin *stringere* meaning "to bind tightly." The word strain derives from the same Latin word. This being the case, it would be easy to suppose that stress and strain might be one and the same thing. However, the term strain tends to be used in connection with unusual tension in a muscle caused by overuse, or because of a sudden or unaccustomed movement. (A strain is a milder injury than a *sprain* in which ligaments around a joint are pulled or torn and swelling occurs).

Examples of how teachers used the word strain in describing stress were:

Stress is:
  mental strain from problems in a person's environment.
  strain caused by a source known or unknown.
  strain on physical and mental well-being.
  excess strain on the body.

The key words *anxiety, emotion,* and *fatigue* were each used by six percent of the teachers to describe their concept of stress. In our previous description of anxiety it was indicated that it should not necessarily be considered the same as stress, but rather that it might be thought of as a combination of certain emotional patterns, principally anger and fear, that can place one in a condition that can bring about stress. Typically, teachers used the term anxiety in connection with their concept of stress as follows:

Stress is:
  demands made on the body caused by anxiety.
  an anxiety reaction.

As far as the key word *emotion* is concerned, it has often been used interchangeably with *stress* in the literature presumably to mean the same thing. As regards their concepts of stress some teachers used the term emotion as follows:
Stress is:
a positive or negative emotional experience.
upsetting the emotions.
a condition that causes emotional rather than logical reactions.
outside emotional influences.
The six percent of the respondents who used the term *fatigue* in expressing their concept of stress, ordinarily described stress as follows:
Stress is:
unnecessary fatigue caused by unpleasant situations.
that point of mental and physical fatigue beyond human capacity.
continuous bombardment which fatigues an individual.
In summarizing the responses of teachers regarding their concepts of stress, two rather interesting bits of information emerged. First, relatively few teachers saw any aspect of stress as positive. That is, the responses were predominantly of a nature that conceived stress as always being undesirable with little or no positive effects. Second, in a large percentage of cases, teachers' concepts of stress tended to focus upon the stressor rather than the condition of stress itself. This would appear to be natural since it has been only in relatively recent years that literature describing what stress is and how it affects the human organism has become more plentiful. At any rate, the responses of teachers about their concept of stress provided the authors with certain important guidelines in preparing the content of this book.

Chapter 2

STATUS OF TEACHER STRESS

STRESS! It's the worst health problem you have to deal with. (78) This was a major conclusion drawn from the Teacher Health Survey conducted by *Instructor* magazine. A typical response of one teacher among several thousand who answered the inquiry was: "Within a limited space I am expected to interact with 30 immature youngsters continuously for six hours a day, five days a week. I am expected to function efficiently in a situation that must reconcile my personal expectations of parents, students, administrators, and fellow staff members. It's not surprising, then, that I feel the negative effects of stress." (37)

The survey revealed that teachers averaged four and one half days of absence each year because of illness, with 33 percent of such absence related to stress. In addition 35 percent of those responding indicated that they had called in sick for reasons of fatigue or nervous strain. Forty percent said that they take prescription drugs, while seven percent indicated that they had had psychiatric treatment. A striking 84 percent believed that there are health hazards in teaching. Moreover, 80 percent said that their view of teaching had changed since they began in the profession. With regard to the seasonal factor of health, 22 percent said they had poor to fair health during the school year, but this figure dropped to four percent during the summer months. And finally—an important statistic as far as this book is concerned—23 percent admitted to poor to fair ability to cope with stress. With teachers themselves declaring that stress is their biggest health problem, it becomes an area of study that might well be considered one of the most important in the whole field of education.

UNIQUENESS OF THE PROFESSION

Job stress has been defined as a lack of harmony between the individual and his work environment. (64) This is a general description that applies to all occupations and professions. The teaching profession is unique, and as such, is concerned with certain stress-related conditions more or less peculiar to this particular profession.

There are numerous factors that make the profession of teaching somewhat unique. Teachers themselves in years past have been considered a unique breed. In fact, although teachers may be thought of as "human beings" in modern times, at one time they were considered by some to be somewhat unlike their fellow man—a "third sex," so to speak. This stereotype has changed appreciably for the better, but nonetheless still persists in certain cases. Although some have designated teaching as the "greatest calling," others subscribe to George Bernard Shaw's "He who can, does, and he who cannot, teaches."

It has been estimated that teachers typically make more than 400 decisions a day. They dispense acceptance, rejection, praise, and reproof on a wholesale basis. (14) It is doubtful that many occupations or professions can lay claim to such a "distinction."

It is sobering to think that any one of these many decisions might have either a short or long range positive or negative influence upon a given student.

The average age of teachers is somewhat lower than that of other professions. Currently, the average is 33 years, the lowest it has ever been. Only about 14 percent of teachers have more than 20 years of service, and only 60 percent of them plan to remain in teaching until retirement. Some reasons given for this are negative student attitude and discipline, incompetent administration, and heavy work load, all of which are stress-provoking conditions. (74)

There are few professions as open to such intense public

scrutiny. Perhaps a part of the reason for this is the constant flow of information from students in schools to their
parents. According to an annual Gallop Poll of the "Public's Attitude Toward the Public Schools," in a four-year
period the quality of education has declined as perceived
by adults in the United States. (87)

The teaching profession may be one of the highest risk
areas as far as violence is concerned. During a school year,
the National Education Association has estimated that
some 65,000 classroom teachers are physically attacked
by students. In a survey of incidents on public school prop-
erty the Senate Juvenile Delinquency Subcommittee reported that in one three-year period murders increased by
19 percent; rapes by 40 percent; robberies by 37 percent;
and assaults on teachers by 77 percent. Moreover it is estimated that thousands of teachers will continue to be
threatened, harassed and physically assaulted. They will
become aware of their personal danger and vulnerability.
They will become fearful and develop stress-related symptoms that will affect them psychologically and physically.
(7) In fact, the problem of violence has become so pronounced that some teacher education institutions are con-
ducting seminars on the topic of "teacher survival," one
purpose of which is to try to provide information on the
teacher's role in attempting to cope with violence.

Another more or less unique aspect of the teaching profession is that although a teacher works with a group of students, a high level of sensitivity must be maintained for each
individual in the group. The qualified teacher is aware that
every student is almost incredibly unique and that he or she
approaches all of the learning tasks with his or her own level
of motivation, capacity, experience and vitality. The teacher
then, by a combination of emotional and logical appeal, attempts to help each student find his or her way through the
experience at his or her own rate, and to some extent in his or
her own way. All of this, of course, while dealing with a relatively large group of individuals.

√ Another factor that tends to set teaching apart from other professions is its criteria for success. In most professions success tends to be measured by the amount of financial remuneration one receives from the job. If this were used as a criterion for success in teaching it is unlikely that many teachers could qualify as successful.

Over the years there have been numerous attempts to identify objectively those characteristics of successful teachers that set them apart from average or poor teachers. Obviously, this is a difficult matter because of the countless variables involved. It is entirely possible for two teachers to possess the same degree of intelligence, preparation, and understanding of the subjects they teach. Yet, it is also possible that one of these teachers will consistently achieve good results with students, while the other will not have much success. Perhaps a good part of the reason for this difference in success lies in those individual differences in personality that influence how teachers deal and interact with students. Based upon the available research and numerous interviews with both teachers and students, we have found that the following characteristics tend to emerge most often among successful teachers: (34)

1. Successful teachers possess those characteristics which in one way or another have a humanizing effect on students. An important factor that good teachers have that appeals to most students is a sense of humor. One third-grade boy put it this way: "She laughed when we played a joke on her."

2. In practically all cases successful teachers are fair and democratic in their dealings with students and they tend to maintain the same positive feelings toward the so-called "problem" student as they do with other students.

3. A very important characteristic is that successful teachers are able to relate easily to students. They have the ability and sensitivity to *listen through students' ears and see through students' eyes.*

4. Successful teachers are flexible. They know that dif-

ferent approaches need to be used with different groups of students as well as individual students. In addition, good teachers can adjust easily to changing situations.
5. Successful teachers are creative. This is an extremely important factor for teachers at the elementary school level because they deal with a very imaginative segment of the population.
6. Successful teachers have control. Different teachers exercise control in different ways, but good teachers tend to have a minimum of control problems probably because of the learning environment they provide.

It would seem to follow that the more successful a teacher is, the less stress he or she might encounter. Although this may generally be the case, it is not always necessarily true. For example, successful teachers put themselves under stress by having the courage to think up and work on new ideas rather than maintaining the *status quo.* Successful teachers tend to worry about their students and as a consequence suffer various degrees of undesirable stress because of this. On the other hand, some of this stress may be necessary and desirable, especially when a teacher experiences the exhilaration of knowing that a student has learned thanks to the teacher's willingness to meet a challenging situation.

RESEARCH ON STRESS IN TEACHING

Although stress as an important dimension in teaching has just recently begun to receive widespread attention, it has been an area of research by some educators for decades. Comparatively speaking, however, this area of research has not received anywhere near the attention it has deserved. In other words, compared to such concerns as *methods of teaching* and *knowledge of subject matter*, one might say that research into stress-related factors in teaching has been minimal. This is somewhat of a paradox, because for years many educators have maintained that personality dynamics and behavior have been among the most important factors in the teaching-learning process. Nevertheless, as mentioned previously, some research in this particular area has taken place over a long period of years, and we will report on some representative examples of these studies here. We will arbitrarily classify these studies into the interrelated and interdependent areas of (a) rate of occurrence of stress in teaching, (b) stress inducing factors in teaching, (c) effects of stress on teaching, and (d) techniques for coping with stress.

Rate of Occurrence of Stress in Teachers

One of the first studies concerned with rate of occurrence of stress in teachers was conducted in the early 1930s. This survey of 600 teachers revealed that 17 percent were *unusually nervous* and that 11 percent had had nervous breakdowns. (33) In a 1938 survey by the National Education Association of over 5,000 teachers it was shown that 37.5 percent of them classified themselves as *seriously worried and nervous.* (56) In another study of 2,200 teachers in 1951 by the National Education Association it was found that 43 percent of the teachers responded that they worked under *considerable strain and tension.* (57) Some 15 years later another National Education Association study of nearly 2,300 teachers found that 16.2 percent said that they worked under *moderate strain.* (58)

It is easy to discern that for many years there has been a relatively high rate of stress in teachers. The fact that this condition may be getting worse is shown in our own very recent studies, which have revealed large percentages of teachers reported that they currently work under stressful conditions.

Stress-Inducing Factors in Teaching

Over the past 40 years, a few studies have attempted to identify factors that induce stress in teachers. As might be expected, these factors encompass a wide range of possibilities, some of which are specific while others are of a general nature. One problem with these studies, it has been observed, lies in the difficulty of determining from the data those specific situations or combinations of situations that result in stress; and further, survey studies usually cannot establish functional relationships between events and behavior. (15) In summarizing the research reported in this area along with our own extensive surveys, certain general classifications of stress-inducing factors tend to emerge. Included among these are (a) self-concerns which induce stress, (b) general working conditions, (c) actions of administrators, (d) actions of colleagues, (e) actions of parents, and (f) behaviors of students.

Effects of Stress on Teaching

Although large numbers of teachers indicate that they work under stressful conditions, it has been difficult to determine objectively the extent to which these conditions, either positively or negatively, influence their teaching. However, attempts have been made to study this feature and a couple of examples of such studies are reported here.

One study found no relationship between teacher anxiety and teaching competence as judged by ratings of supervisors. (62) However, another study revealed that student ratings of effectiveness of teaching were the highest for teachers who had a low-anxiety level. (48) In summarizing a number of studies in this area, the generalization could perhaps be made that stressful teaching conditions may result in various degrees of lower level teaching performance.

Techniques of Coping with Stress

Studies to determine the value of stress-coping strategies for teachers have met with varying, and in some cases, contradictory results. A major reason for this is that it is an extremely difficult area to study objectively. The lack of validity and reliability of some of the measuring instruments, along with the problem of controlling numerous variables, contribute to the difficulty of a purely scientific approach. In spite of this, some notable researchers, such as Drs. Thomas Coates and Carl Thoresen, report that promising results, backed up by research, have been obtained from methods based on systematic desensitization and relaxation techniques. (15) (The use of these as well as other techniques for coping with stress will be recommended in subsequent chapters).

It should be mentioned that a lack of solid evidence to support the use of certain coping techniques should not necessarily preclude their use by teachers. This is to say that there may be sufficient empirical evidence to justify consideration of the various coping techniques on a selected basis to meet the particular needs of individual teachers.

The studies that we have reported in this discussion represent a sampling of the research carried out in this area over a period of several decades beginning in the early 1930s. Our own accumulation of data, alluded to previously, is kept up to date on an ongoing basis. Various aspects of this information will be incorporated into different sections of the book. However, it may be appropriate to report on it generally at this point. It should be mentioned that our surveys did not involve a scientific sample; however the data provided us with a substantial amount of information regarding stress in teaching. The work was extensive in that we surveyed teachers at all levels from the elementary school through the university. In addition, most all of the areas of specialization were sampled including teachers of art, music, and physical education, as well as teachers of the mentally retarded. The teachers surveyed included those from inner-city, suburban, and rural areas.

Inasmuch as this book is concerned essentially with public school teachers below the college level our greatest emphasis was placed on these. Our findings tended to show that, generally speaking, stress-inducing factors did not differ greatly across the combination of areas surveyed. However, there were certain stress-inducing factors peculiar to certain segments of the sample. For instance, among physical education teachers a unique stress-inducing factor was "complying with Title IX," which deals with integration of the sexes in physical education classes. Unique at the level of college teaching was the stress brought about by what the large majority of college teachers labeled "continuing impingement on academic freedom." Although public-school teachers saw administrators and administrative practices as a major stress-inducing factor, this appeared to be much more pronounced among college teachers. Many college teachers felt that they were placed under stress because of what was described generally as a "lack of scholarly achievement among college administrators." The generally prevailing feeling seemed to be that at the college level administrators were in such positions because of their inability to carry out functions which require scholarly achievement.

WHAT TEACHERS ARE DOING TO COPE WITH STRESS

One dimension of our surveys of stress among teachers was concerned with what teachers are currently doing to cope with stress. It was felt that if such information were available it would provide some guidance for making suggestions and recommendations. These data, derived from teachers at all grade levels and in most all of the subject areas, are summarized in the following discussion. Incidentally, the results tend to reveal a critical need for the type of information provided in this book.

One rather disturbing statistic revealed that 49 percent of the respondents indicated that they were more or less at a loss on how to deal with stress. A common response was to "grin and bear it" and many in this classification felt that this caused more stress. Many others said that they "tried to forget" but that this did not help.

In 16 percent of the cases *discussion with others* was a procedure for coping. In a subsequent section of the book this practice is stated as a general principle that teachers might apply in management of stress. Included among those with whom problems were discussed were peers, spouses, administrators, parents, and psychologists.

Nine percent of the respondents resorted to some sort of *divine guidance* with a majority in this category saying that they prayed and applied the principles that the Bible teaches. It may be of interest to note that a very large number of the responses in this group came from teachers in rural areas.

In seven percent of the cases the important practice of *setting tasks* in the right order of priority was applied by reexamining practices when pressure builds, organizing daily routine, and planning well ahead.

Another seven percent used physical exercise as a method of coping, and this included running, biking, and weight training. Most of those in this category were physical education teachers who were perhaps more aware of the value of exercise.

Six percent resorted to drugs and various forms of medication. They were about equally divided in the use of prescription drugs, and non-prescription drugs, while a number resorted to the use of alcoholic beverages.

Three percent used recreational activities as a coping measure, and these pursuits included reading at home, leisure work at home, and sports and games. Of the two percent who used *meditation* as a means of coping, all of these respondents reported great success with this technique and recommended it for all teachers. Only one percent used *progressive relaxation* to cope with stress, although this has been considered one of the most important coping procedures over the years.

CHAPTER 3

WHAT TEACHERS SHOULD KNOW ABOUT STRESS

One of the first steps to take in dealing satisfactorily with stress is to acquire some degree of knowledge about the subject. Therefore, it is the function of this chapter to provide the reader with a general overview of some of the many aspects of stress.

THEORIES OF STRESS

It should be mentioned at this point that it is not our intent to get into a highly technical discourse on the complex and complicated nature of stress. However, there are certain basic understandings that need to be taken into account and this requires the use of certain technical terms. For this reason it appears appropriate to provide an "on-the-spot" glossary of terms used in the discussion to follow.

ACTH—(adrenocorticotropic hormone) Secreted by the pituitary gland. It influences the function of the adrenals and other glands in the body.

adrenalin—A hormone secreted by the medulla of the adrenal glands.

adrenals—Two glands in the upper posterior part of the abdomen that produce and secrete hormones. They have two parts, the outer layer, called the *cortex*, and the inner core, called the *medulla*.

corticoids—Hormones produced by the adrenal cortex, an example of which is *cortisone*.

hormone—A chemical produced by a gland, secreted into the blood stream, and influencing the function of cells or organs.

hypothalamus—The primary activator of the autonomic nervous system, it plays a central role in

23

translating neurological stimuli into endocrine processes during stress reaction.

pituitary—An endocrine gland located at the base of the brain, about the size of a pea. It secretes important hormones, one of which is ACTH.

thymus—A ductless gland that is considered a part of the endocrine gland system, located behind the upper part of the breast bone.

Although there are various theories concerned with the nature of stress, one of the better known and widely accepted is that of the previously mentioned Dr. Hans Selye. (70) We have already given Selye's description of stress as the "nonspecific response of the body to any demand." The physiological processes and the reactions involved in Selye's stress model have become known as the *General Adaptation Syndrome* and consists of the three stages of *alarm reaction, resistance stage* and the *exhaustion stage.*

In the first stage (alarm reaction) the body reacts to the stressor and causes the hypothalamus to produce a biochemical "messenger" which in turn causes the pituitary gland to secrete ACTH into the blood. This hormone then causes the adrenal gland to discharge adrenalin and other corticoids. This causes shrinkage of the thymus with an influence on heart rate, blood pressure and the like. It is during the alarm stage that the resistance of the body is reduced.

In the second stage, *resistance* develops if the stressor is not too pronounced. Body adaptation develops to fight back the stress or possibly avoid it and the body begins to repair damage, if any.

The third stage of *exhaustion* occurs if there is long-continued exposure to the same stressor. The ability of the adaptation is eventually exhausted and the signs of the first stage (alarm reaction) reappear. Selye contended that our adaptation resources are limited and when they become irreversible the result is death. (Our objective, of course, should be to keep our resistance and capacity for adaptation, and this is a good part of what this book is about. In later chapters various coping strategies and possible preventive measures for stress will be suggested for teachers).

As mentioned before, Selye's stress model, which places emphasis upon "nonspecific" responses, has been widely accepted over the years. However, recently the nonspecific nature of stress has been questioned by some. In this connection, reference is made to the brilliant research of Dr. John W. Mason of Yale University, a former President of the American Psychosomatic Society. His findings tend to support the idea that other hormones are involved in stress in addition to those of the pituitary-adrenal system. (47) Dr. Mason's data suggest that psychological stressors activate other endocrine systems in addition to those activated by physiological stressors such as cold, electric shock, and the like.

As with all research, the search for truth will continue and more and more precise and sophisticated procedures will emerge in the scientific study of stress. Current theories will be more critically appraised and evaluated and other theories are likely to be advanced. In the meantime, there is abundant evidence to support the notion that stress in modern society can be a most serious threat to the well-being of man, if not controlled, and of course the most important factor in such control is man himself.

REACTIONS TO STRESS

There are various ways in which reactions to stress may be classified, and in any kind of classification there will be some degree of unavoidable overlapping. In this discussion we will arbitrarily suggest two broad classifications as *physiological* and *behavioral*.

Physiological Reactions

Although all individuals do not always react in the same way physiologically to stress, the following generalized list suggests some of the more or less standard body reactions.

1. Rapid beating of the heart, sometimes described as "pounding of the heart." Most everyone has experienced this reaction at one time or another as a result of great excitement, or in the case of being afraid.

2. Perspiration, mostly of the palms of the hands although there may be profuse sweating in some individuals at various other parts of the body.

3. The blood pressure rises: this may be referred to as a hidden reaction because the individual is not likely to be aware of it.

4. The pupils of the eyes may dilate, and again the individual will not necessarily be aware of this.

5. The stomach seems to "knot up" and this is sometimes referred to as "feeling a lump in the pit of the stomach." This of course can have a negative influence on digestion.

6. Sometimes individuals experience difficulty in swallowing, which is often characterized as a "lump in the throat."

7. There may be a tight feeling in the chest and when the stressful condition is relieved one may refer to it as "getting a load off of my chest."

What these various bodily reactions mean is that the organism is gearing up for a response to a stressor. This phenomenon is called the *fight or flight* response and was first described as an *emergency reaction* by Dr. Walter B. Cannon, the famous Harvard University Professor of Physiology, a good many years ago. (12) The fight or flight response prepares a person for action in the same way that it did for prehistoric man when he was confronted with an enemy. His response was decided on the basis of the particular situation, such as fighting an opponent for food or fleeing from an animal for which he was no match. In modern times with all of the potentially stressful conditions provoking a fight or flight response, modern man uses these same physiological responses to face up to these kinds of situations. In general, however, people today do not need to fight physically (although they might feel like it sometimes), or to run from wild animals. But a person's body still reacts with the same fight or flight response. Physiologists point out that people still need this means of self-preservation on occasion, but not in response to the emotional traumas and anxieties of modern living.

✓ *Behavioral Reactions*

In discussing behavioral reactions it should be mentioned again that various degrees of unavoidable overlapping may occur between these reactions and physiological reactions. Although behavioral reactions are for the most part physically oriented, they are likely to involve more overt manifestations that are provoked by the physiological reactions. For purposes of this discussion we will consider *behavior* to mean anything that the organism does as a result of some sort of stimulation.

An individual under stress will function with a behavior that is different from ordinary behavior. We will arbitrarily subclassify these as (a) *counter* behavior (sometimes referred to as defensive behavior), (b) *dysfunctional* behavior, and (c) *overt* behavior (sometimes referred to as expressive behavior).

In *counter* behavior a person will sometimes take action that is intended to counteract the stressful condition. For example, a teacher might counter a situation by shouting at a student who has stimulated a stressful situation by committing an act that is not acceptable to the teacher. Incidentally, some studies show that this kind of behavior on the part of the teacher may be associated with less successful teaching, (88) and also that it might make students more disruptive. (45)

Another example of counter behavior is that of an individual taking a defensive position, such as a teacher avoiding a particular unacceptable act of a student. This may be a satisfactory approach on the part of the teacher because a general recommendation for beginning teachers has been for them to ignore inappropriate behavior while positively attending to desired behavior. Although this approach can result in the reduction of inappropriate behavior, it might have an adverse affect on the anxiety level of the teacher. For example, if a teacher is already under stress in a given teaching situation this might become more pronounced when a teacher ignores inappropriate behavior. Of course, this is contingent upon the degree of acceptability of the student behavior.

A final example of counter behavior is the teacher practicing an "on-the-spot" relaxation technique but at the same time being unaware of it. That is, the teacher might take a deep breath and silently "count to ten" before taking action, if any.

Dysfunctional behavior refers to a reaction that demonstrates impaired or abnormal functioning and that results in a lower level of skill performance than one is ordinarily capable of accomplishing. There might be changes in the normal speech patterns and this could be accompanied by an inability to function well mentally. There could be a temporary impairment of the systems of perception as well as temporary loss of memory. Many teachers have experienced this at one time or another due to a stress-inducing situation, as for example with a "mental block" where the attempt to get back on to the original train of thought causes some degree of frustration.

Overt behavior involves such reactions as distorted facial expressions like tics and twitches, and biting the lip. There appears to be a need for the person to move about,

and thus pacing around the room is characteristic. Incidentally, there is a point of view that suggests that overt behavior in the form of activity is preferable for most individuals in most stressful situations and that it can be highly
effective in reducing threat and distress. (30)

Another form of overt behavior is skin flushing, or blush-
ing. This is manifested by many teachers and it can sometimes become the objective of high-school age boys to
make a young attractive female teacher blush. Indeed, students are often quick to discern these overt behavioral
mannerisms and sometimes diligently work on them to
"get old lady so-and-so's goat." Obviously, this suggests
that the remedy might be in an attempt at some sort of behavior modification on the part of the teacher, and this will
be discussed in detail in a later chapter.

CLASSIFICATIONS OF STRESS

The difficulty encountered in attempting to devise a
foolproof classification system for the various kinds of
stress should be obvious. The reason for this of course lies
in the fact that it is practically impossible to fit a given type
of stress neatly into one exclusive category. As we found in
attempting to classify *reactions* to stress in the immediately
preceding section of the chapter, we are again confronted
with the problem of overlap when we try to classify various
kinds of stress. However, an attempt will be made to do so,
and, as has been mentioned before, any such classification
on our part is purely arbitrary. Others may wish to use different classifications, and in the absence of anything re-
sembling standardization, it is their prerogative to do so.
With this general idea in mind, the classifications of stress
that we will deal with in the following discussion are (a) undesirable, (b) desirable, (c) physical, (d) psychological, (e)
emotional, (f) social, (g) occupational, and (h) environmental. It should be understood that this does not exhaust the

possibilities of various kinds of stress classifications. That is, this particular listing is not necessarily theoretically complete, but for our purposes it should suffice.

Undesirable Stress

In the literature, undesirable stress may be referred to as *distress*. In this regard, it is interesting to note that Selye refers to the pleasant or healthy kind of stress as "eustress," and to the unpleasant or unhealthy kind as "distress." (72)

As the reader will see later, stress has some desirable features, but like any factor involving the human organism, most anything in excess is harmful. And, of course, this holds true for abnormal amounts of stress. When stress becomes prolonged, unrelenting, and thus chronic, it can result in very serious trouble. It is a well documented fact that emotional upset caused by anger, fear and the like, and stored up over a period of time can be a dangerous threat to health. It has been suggested that what has ordinarily been referred to as *aging* is nothing more than the sum total of all the scars left by the stress of life. This could be the reason why some comparatively young persons are said to "look old for their years." In the final analysis the recommendation is not necessarily to avoid stress but to keep it from becoming a chronic condition.

Desirable Stress

The classic comment by Selye that "stress is the spice of life" (72) perhaps sums up the general idea that stress can be desirable as well as devastating. He goes on to say that the only way one could avoid stress would be to never do anything, and that certain kinds of activities have a beneficial influence in keeping the stress mechanism in good shape.

Certainly, the human organism needs to be taxed in order to function well, and it is a well-known physiological fact that muscles will soon atrophy if not subjected to sufficient use. It is somewhat like the family car—it will soon rust and deteriorate if left unused. Athletes express a desirable aspect of stress when they talk about the exhilarating feeling of "getting up" for a game, and the feeling of the "juices flowing."

At one time or another almost everyone has experienced "butterflies in the stomach" when faced with a particularly challenging situation. In the case of a teacher, the excitement of seeing a student learn can be an exhilarating experience and leave one with the joyous feeling of a job well done. In this regard, the great 19th-century educator, Horace Mann once remarked, "I have seen a teacher clap his hands for joy when a boy of 12 has made a bright answer." (70) Thus, it is important that we understand that stress is a perfectly normal human state and that the organism is under various degrees of stress in those conditions that are related to happiness as well as those concerned with sadness.

Although both "good" stress and "bad" stress reactions place specific demands for resources on the body, does this mean that good stress is "safe" and bad stress "dangerous?" Two prominent psychologists, Drs. Israel Posner and Lewis Leitner have some interesting suggestions in this regard. They feel that two psychological variables, *predictability* and *controllability* play an important role. (66)

It can be reasoned that *predictable* pain and discomfort is less stressful because under this condition a person is said to be capable of learning when it is safe to "lower his guard" and relax. Since periods of impending pain are clearly signaled, the person can safely relax at times when the warning signal is absent. These periods of psychological safety seem to insulate individuals from harmful effects of stress. Obviously, persons receiving unsignaled pain have no way of knowing when it is safe to relax and thus are more likely to develop serious health problems as a result of chronic psychological stress.

The second psychological variable, *controllability* of environmental stressors, which is closely related to coping behavior, also plays a major part in determining stress effects. However, such coping behavior is beneficial if a person is given a feedback signal which informs him that the coping response was successful in avoiding an impending stressor. Without the feedback success, active coping behavior, as such, may increase stress effects, since it calls upon the energy reserves of the body and leaves it in a state of chronic stress.

The research on predictability and controllability of stressful events may help to explain why it is that people who seek out stressful and challenging activities do not appear to develop stress related illnesses: because typically the events associated with it are planned in advance (they are predictable) or otherwise scheduled or integrated (they are controlled) into the individual's life. However, even activities that are generally considered pleasant and exciting (good stress) can produce illness if the individual is not forewarned or has little control over the events. And, unpleasant events (bad stress) may result in stress-related illness because they generally come without warning and cannot be controlled.

Stress, then, can be viewed positively as a challenge or negatively as a threat. It can be a friend or foe. Stress, when managed successfully, may contribute to a fulfilling life. When approached seriously, it can be a system of preventive maintenance or enhancement. It exists as a fact of life, most often in work settings and family environments. Those who have learned to manage it and channel it wisely find it to be a thriving force in their lives. A secret to its effective utilization is the knowledge of the point in time when it no longer produces pleasant, satisfying, and positive reactions and threatens to move in a negative direction, draining the reactant of more psychic, physical and emotional energy than he or she is able to give. (46)

Some have taken the middle ground on this subject by saying that stress is neither good *nor* bad, indicating that the effect of stress is not determined by the stress itself but how it is viewed and handled. That is, one either handles stress properly or allows it to influence the organism negatively, thus making one a victim of undesirable stress.

Physical Stress

In discussing physical stress it might be well to differentiate between the two terms *physical* and *physiological*. The former should be considered a broad term and it can be described as "pertaining to or relating to the body." On the other hand, the term *physiological* is concerned with what the organs of the body do in relation to each other. Thus, physical stress could be concerned with unusual and excessive physical exertion as well as certain physiological conditions brought about by some kind of stress.

Although there are many kinds of physical stress, they can perhaps be separated into two general types, to which the organism may react in different ways. One type may be referred to as *emergency* stress and the other as *continuing* stress. In emergency stress the previously described physiological phenomenon takes place. That is, when an emergency arises such as a bodily injury, hormones are discharged into the blood stream. This involves increase in heart rate, rise in blood pressure, along with dilation of the blood vessels in the muscles to prepare themselves for immediate use of the energy that is generated.

In continuing stress the bodily reaction is somewhat more complex. The physiological involvement is the same, but more and more hormones continue to be produced, the purpose of which is to increase body resistance. In cases where the stress is excessive, such as an extensive third-degree burn, a third phase in the form of exhaustion of the adrenal glands can develop, sometimes culminating in fatal results.

It was mentioned that physical stress can also be related to unusual and excessive physical exertion. This can be depicted in a general way through an experiment involving some more or less mild physical exertion. First, try to find your resting pulse. This can be done by placing your right wrist, palm facing you, in your left hand. Now, bring the index and middle fingers of your left hand around the wrist and press slightly until you feel the beat of your pulse. Next, time this beat for ten seconds and then multiply this figure by six. This will give your resting pulse rate per minute. For example, if you counted 12 beats in the ten seconds, your resting pulse will be 72 beats per minute. The next step is to engage in some physical activity. Stand and balance yourself on one foot. Hop up and down on this foot for a period of about 30 seconds, or less if it is too strenuous. Take your pulse rate again in the same manner as suggested above. You will find that as a result of this activity your pulse will be elevated above your resting pulse. Even with this small amount of physical exertion, the body was adjusting to cope with it, as evidenced by the rise in pulse rate. This was discernible to you; however, other things of which you were not aware, such as a slight rise in blood pressure, are likely to have been involved.

Psychological Stress

The essential difference between physical stress and psychological stress is that the former involves a real situation, while psychological stress is more concerned with foreseeing or imagining an emergency situation. As an example, a vicarious experience of danger may be of sufficient intensity to cause muscle tension and elevate the heart rate. A specific example of psychological stress is seen in what is commonly called "stage fright." Incidentally, it is interesting to note that this type of psychological stress may start when one is a child. For example, our studies of stress-inducing factors in children have indicated that "getting up in front of the class" is an incident that causes much concern and worry to a large number of children. (36)

Prolonged and unrelenting nervous tension developing from psychological stress can result in psychosomatic disorders which in turn can cause various serious diseases.

Emotional Stress

Emotional stress can be brought about by the stimulus of any of the emotional patterns. For example, the emotional pattern of anger can be stimulated by such factors as the thwarting of one's wishes, or a number of cumulative irritations. Responses to such stimuli can be either *impulsive* or *inhibited*. An impulsive expression of anger is one that is directed against a person or an object, while the inhibited expressions are kept under control and may be manifested by such overt behaviors as skin flushing.

Generally speaking, emotional patterns can be placed into the two broad categories of *pleasant* emotions and *unpleasant* emotions. Pleasant emotional patterns include such things as joy, affection, happiness, and love in the broad sense, while included among the unpleasant emotional patterns are anger, sorrow, jealousy, fear, and worry—an imaginary form of fear.

At one time or another everyone has manifested emotional behavior as well as ordinary behavior. Differences in the structure of the organism and in the environment will largely govern the degree to which each individual expresses emotional behavior. Moreover, it has been suggested that the pleasantness or unpleasantness of an emotion seems to be determined by its strength and intensity, ɘ nature of the situation arousing it, and by the way ᴛʜᴇ ᴵⁿdividual perceives or interprets the situation.

The ancient Greeks identified emotions with certain organs of the body. For example, in general, sorrow was expressed from the heart (a broken heart); jealousy was associated with the liver; hate with the gall bladder and anger with the spleen. In regard to the latter, we sometimes hear the expression "venting one's spleen" on someone. We make this historical reference because in modern times we take into account certain principal conduits between the motions and the body. These are by way of the nervous system and the endocrine system. That part of the nervous system principally concerned with the emotions is the autonomic nervous system which controls functions such as the heartbeat, blood pressure, and digestion. When there is a stimulus of any of the emotional patterns these two systems activate in the manner previously explained. By way of illustration, if the emotional pattern of fear is stimulated the heartbeat accelerates, breathing is more rapid and the blood pressure is likely to rise. Energy fuel is discharged into the blood from storage in the liver which causes the blood sugar level to rise. These, along with other bodily functions serve to prepare the person to cope with the condition caused by the fear. He then reacts with the fight or flight response discussed earlier.

In view of the fact that emotionality is such an important factor in teaching, it seems appropriate at this point to mention some of the characteristics of emotionally healthy teachers. Looking at these characteristics it must be recognized that they are not absolute nor are they static. Teachers are not always happy, and they sometimes find themselves in situations where they are not overly confident. In fact sometimes they may feel downright inadequate to solve certain commonplace daily problems that occur in the classroom.

1. Emotionally healthy teachers have achieved basic harmony within themselves and a workable relationship

with colleagues and students. They are able to function effectively and most of the time happily, even though they are well aware of the limitations and rigors involved in human existence.

2. Emotionally healthy teachers manage to adapt to the demands of teaching conditions with emotional responses that are appropriate in degree and kind to the stimuli or situations and that fall generally within the range of what is considered "normal" for the school environment.

3. Emotionally healthy teachers face problems directly and seek realistic and plausible solutions to them. They try to free themselves from excessive and unreal anxieties, worries, and fears even though they are aware that there is much to be concerned with and much to be anxious about in the teaching profession in modern times.

4. Emotionally healthy teachers have developed a guiding philosophy of life and have a set of values that are acceptable to themselves and that are generally in harmony with those values of society which are reasonable and conducive to human happiness.

5. Emotionally healthy teachers accept themselves and are willing to deal with the world as it exists in reality. They accept what cannot be changed at a particular time and place and they build and derive satisfaction within the framework of their own potentialities and those of their teaching environment.

6. Emotionally healthy teachers tend to be happy, and they tend to have an enthusiasm for living, and for teaching. They do not focus their attention exclusively upon what they consider to be their inadequacies, weaknesses, and "bad" qualities. They view those around them—students and colleagues—in this way too.

7. Emotionally healthy teachers have a variety of satisfying interests and maintain a balance between their job of teaching, routine responsibilities, and recreation. They find constructive and satisfying outlets for creative

expression in teaching and outside interests that they undertake.

This list of characteristics of emotionally healthy teachers presents a near-ideal situation and obviously none of them operate at these high levels at all times. However, they might well be regarded as suitable guidelines, for which teachers might strive, to assist them in dealing with unpleasant emotional stress.

Social Stress

Human beings are social beings. They do things together. They play together. They work together for the benefit of society. They have fought together in time of national emergency in order to preserve the kind of society in which they believe. This means that life involves a constant series of social interactions, in which the individual has some sort of impact upon society, and society in turn has an influence upon the individual.

There are obviously many levels of social stress in life situations. For example, economic conditions and other special problems have been found to be very stressful situations for many people. Social stress for teachers for purposes of this discussion will be confined to the daily social roles in the school situation.

In teaching, the emphasis tends to be placed on the team approach. The teaching staff is sometimes referred to as a team, or the staff members as good team members. And, in some instances there is involvement in "team teaching." All the previously mentioned social interactions are characterized by attitudes which can be classified as *positive, negative,* or *neutral.* Social interactions with students, colleagues, administrators, and parents that involve a positive attitude are most likely to meet with success in avoiding social stress. In dealing with students, teachers have found particular value in what has been termed *positive rein-*

forcement. One example of positive reinforcement in social interaction with a student might be to emphasize the number of times a student answered correctly on a test rather than putting emphasis on the number of items that were incorrect.

Negative attitudes about social interactions will almost always generate hard feelings and hostility among staff members and make teaching a more difficult task, and thus more stressful for all concerned. A neutral or *laissez faire* attitude often degenerates into one of tolerance, and as such can become almost as devastating as a negative attitude. In fact, the development of an "I don't care" attitude can often make life on the job of teaching intolerable and bring about stress. In the final analysis, teachers themselves hold the key to avoidance of undesirable social stress in the school situation, and good social relationships are most likely to be obtained if one assumes a positive attitude in such relationships.

Occupational Stress

There are many stress-related conditions connected with one's occupation. And it is well known that some kinds of employment are "highly stressful" and others are considered "relatively stress-free." Various studies comparing such groups have indicated that those in the highly stressful occupations tend to have a higher incidence of serious diseases, presumably resulting from stressful conditions on the job.

Perhaps the secret lies in attempting to obtain a position of employment where one can deal with the stress levels required of that position. The late President Harry Truman characterized this situation with his often quoted statement: "If you can't stand the heat, stay out of the kitchen." In this particular regard, it is interesting to note that it has been shown that persons with low confidence in their competencies are likely to seek relatively secure and undemanding occupations, while those with high self-confidence are more likely to seek more demanding occupations. (43)

Although, as we have said before, there are several studies that have identified stress-inducing factors in teaching, few have been concerned with the extent to which such factors may produce serious harm. However, the potential for such conditions is shown in the previously reported study of more than 9,000 teachers in which it was revealed that "*Stress* is your biggest bugaboo. Tensions and pressure build up, affecting your health and teaching performance. You think you could better cope with stress if you could learn how to leave problems at school; learn that there are limits to what a teacher can do." (37)

There is one study that took into account long-term work stress in teachers and prison guards. (9) Comparing teaching with guarding prisoners may seem remote, but the researcher, Dr. Carroll M. Brodsky suggests that these occupations are more similar than may appear on first consideration. That is, while teachers are in education and prison guards are in criminology, in a larger perspective both serve as caretakers or custodians of persons who are in their charge not by choice, but by law. The study showed that conditions precipitating long-term stress were essentially the same for both groups. These conditions involve dealing with their charges, dealing with co-workers, and dealing with superiors.

In the case of teaching, as well as in various other careers, one is probably not aware of the demands of the job until he or she is actually in it. There is little opportunity to determine the extent of these demands because ordinarily the first actual job contact one gets is in the student teaching experience which usually comes during the final year of teacher preparation. Fortunately, some teacher preparation institutions are trying to improve upon this situation by providing earlier on-the-job experiences, possibly as soon as the second year of college.

Environmental Stress

The term *environment* is so broad that it can be considered to involve any and all circumstances that have some sort of influence on the human organism. That is, it concerns everything that is external to the human organism but that influences it nonetheless. That stress is such a factor is recognized by at least one authority, who defines stress as: "Environmental conditions that require *behavioral adjustment*." (4)

The term environment itself has a host of modifiers, a few of which are home, social, climatic, and of course the one that is the major concern of this book, the school environment. Dependent upon circumstances, these and various other environments contain inherent possibilities for inducing stress.

CAUSES OF STRESS

Throughout our discussions up to this point we have alluded indirectly to various possible causes of stress. There are so many general causes that almost anything that occurs in our life can cause stress to a certain degree. These general causes include, among a host of others, all of the various factors concerned with our modern highly technological society, such as air travel that makes the world a "smaller place," the mass media, especially the daily news that bombards us with information, which if taken too seriously can provide for stressful conditions. In addition, such factors as overcrowding, air and noise pollution, along with the everyday "hustle and bustle to survive" combine to make life in general a somewhat frustrating experience.

Everyone, teachers as well as others, are possible stress victims of the kinds of conditions mentioned above. Moreover, some by the very nature of their specific environment are susceptible to many stress-inducing factors. Such is the case with causes of stress among those in the teaching profession. That is, in addition to the various life events that cause stress, teachers as a group may be more or less uniquely susceptible to stress caused by students, colleagues, administrators, parents and certain aspects of working conditions.

EFFECTS OF STRESS

As in the case of *causes of stress*, we have been alluding indirectly to some of the effects of stress in our previous discussions. It should be recalled that while stress can be detrimental, it can be beneficial as well. Thus, in this discussion we will take into account both its ill effects and its good effects.

One source has reported as a tragic consequence, of increased stress is that stress-related psychological and physiological disorders have become the number-one social and health problem in the last decade, and further, that most standard medical textbooks attribute anywhere from 50 to 80 percent of all diseases to psychosomatic or stress-related origins. (64) Selye has gone so far as to say that stress is involved in *all* diseases by indicating that every disease causes a certain amount of stress, since it imposes demands for adaptation upon the organism. In turn, stress plays some role in the development of every disease; its effects—for better or for worse—are added to the specific changes characteristic of the disease in question. (72)

In a recent review of the literature by various medical authorities we found that among various other conditions, the following in some way could be stress-related: coronary heart disease, diabetes, cirrhosis of the liver, high blood pressure, peptic ulcer, migraine headaches, multiple sclerosis, herpes, lung disease, injury due to accidents, mental breakdown, and even cancer. This is almost to say, "You name it; stress causes it!" (Incidentally, in the case of stress and cancer, it is known that *cortisol* is secreted in greater quantities in response to stress, leading some scientists to believe that cortisol may retard the liver's detoxification of foreign substances including cancer-causing chemicals).

One of the most recent findings has been that there is evidence linking stress with the body's ability to fight disease. Some studies suggest the possibility of immune-system malfunction under stress by comparing the infection-fighting capability of white blood cells taken from normal and from severely stressed individuals.

There is good news, however, some of which is epitomized in the following comment by Arthur S. Freese: "The stress response is still needed for dealing with real threats: a stiff game of tennis and other situations requiring quick action with extra strength; accidents, when stress increases the body's blood-clotting ability, preventing loss of too much blood; speaking up in public, when the alarm reaction brings more oxygen to the brain to help meet the intellectual challenge." (27)

In closing this section of the chapter, it seems important to take into account that there is an ever growing body of knowledge concerned with the relationship between stress and its effects upon the human organism. Some opinions are based of scientific findings and others are not. It is well to remember that simply because a relationship exists between two variables, this should not be mistaken for causation. That is, there may not necessarily be a cause-and-effect relationship, but simply coexisting behaviors. Nonetheless, there is an accumulation of more and more scientific evidence to support what at one time were mere theoretical speculations. It will remain the responsibility of further research to provide more conclusive evidence to support current thinking.

INDIVIDUAL DIFFERENCES AND STRESS

In the field of education we tend to place so much emphasis on individual differences of students that we sometimes forget the individual differences that also exist among teachers. Certainly teachers as well as others differ in many traits and characteristics. Thus, everyone differs with regard to stress. Among other things, people differ in how they respond to stress and how it effects them.

There are a number of classifications of factors of individual difference with regard to stress. We will comment on three of these; that is, the *noxious stimulus factor*, the *sex factor*, and the *personality factor*.

The Noxious Stimulus Factor

Some years ago Dr. Harold G. Wolff, in search of ways in which people react to stress-inducing factors, gave serious concern to what was identified as noxious stimuli. (85) These are the kinds of stimuli that can have a damaging effect on the individual. Wolff believed that a stimulus could be noxious for one individual but not necessarily for another. This is to say that while one stressor may have a devastating effect on one person it may have little or no effect on another.

The Sex Factor

As far as individual differences regarding the sex factor are concerned it is felt generally that with the recent women's movement more females will continue to become more susceptible to stress. Walter McQuade and Ann Aikan point this up specifically by stating that, "There are signs that women's vulnerability is increasing as fast as their independence. A century ago peptic ulcers were a women's ailment, by a ratio of seven to three. Then, as frontier rigors were replaced by industrial ones life got easier for women and harder for men, and from 1920 to 1940 nine out of ten victims were male. But since mid-century the incidence of ulcers in women is again on the rise." (49)

As for stress as a factor in gender longevity there is a general feeling that physiologically men react more intensely to stress than women. This can result in the production of higher levels of adrenalin in male stress reactivity and possibly enhance the aging process.

In an objective approach to the sex factor the first author of this book was the senior researcher on a study of sex individual differences in stress reactivity. (35) A "State Measurement Scale" was used for the purpose of finding out from male and female college students how they generally felt while experiencing a stress response situation.

The study showed that males and females "perceive" different stress reactions. Of greatest disparity between the perceptions of males and females was the emergence of *gastrointestinal sensitivities* (such as upset stomach) exclusively among males and the emergence of an *aversive affective sensitivity* (such as a feeling of being "high strung") exclusively among females.

It was impossible to attach any significance to the appearance of a gastrointestinal sensitivity among males and an affective sensitivity among females. However, it was speculated that socio-cultural factors might have been involved. The reason for this is that it may be socially acceptable for males to develop "executive ulcers." Regarding the affective sensitivity, generally speaking, males are ordinarily taught to repress emotions, and many males perceive emotion as a sign of weakness. Similarly, females have been traditionally taught that it is appropriate for them to demonstrate emotion. As this era of changing sex roles progresses it will be interesting to see if perceptions

of stress responsiveness change as well. If cultural factors
do indeed influence perceptions of responsiveness, one
might be willing to speculate that, eventually, there would
be a more common perception of stress reactions among
males and females.

The Personality Factor

Before commenting on personality as it pertains to individual differences in stress, it seems appropriate to discuss
briefly our conception of personality. Ordinarily, personality is often dealt with only as a psychological entity. We
are tending to think of it here in a broader frame of reference, that is the *total* personality. We view this total personality as consisting of physical, social, emotional and intellectual aspects. This conforms more or less with what is
becoming one rather common description of personality,
which is "existence as a person," and this should be interpreted to mean the whole person, or unified individual.
(The total personality concept will be dealt with in greater
detail in a subsequent chapter).

There appears to be general agreement that personality
can influence the way individuals handle stress. On the
other hand, there is much less agreement regarding personality as a causal factor in disease. One specific example
of this is the difference in opinion regarding the extent to
which certain types of personalities are associated with
heart disease. A case in point concerns the work of Drs.
Meyer Friedman and Ray H. Rosenman, who have designated a Type-A behavior and a Type-B behavior. A person
with Type-A behavior tends to be aggressive, ambitious,
competitive and puts pressure on himself in getting things
done. An individual with Type-B behavior is more easy
going, relaxed, and tends not to put pressure on himself.
With regard to these two types of behavior. Friedman and

Rosenman state, "In the absence of Type-A Behavior Pattern, coronary heart disease almost never occurs before 70 years of age, regardless of the fatty foods eaten, the cigarettes smoked, or the lack of exercise. But when this behavior pattern is present, coronary heart disease can easily erupt in one's 30s or 40s." (29)

This view has come under challenge from some authorities, the main point of contention being that there is little objective scientific evidence to support it. In fact, at a recent American Heart Association forum for science writers it was reported that scientific studies fail to show that stress causes heart attacks. (3) In this connection, it is interesting that many heart specialists have noted that death from heart disease is on a downward trend which may be expected to continue. They credit this, among other things, to improvements in diet, control of high blood pressure, and particularly to exercise.

There is general agreement that one manifests his or her personality through certain behavior traits and characteristics. This being the case, if these traits and characteristics can be positively identified as detrimental to one's health, then it may be possible to modify behaviors that are causing a problem. To date research in this area is difficult to pursue mainly because of the problem of controlling the large number of influencing variables.

It has been the intent of this chapter to familiarize the reader with some of the basic facets and ramifications of stress. For the most part the discussions have been of a general nature, although in some cases specific reference was made to teachers and/or teaching situations. In the subsequent chapters we turn our attention to stress as it is related more specifically to conditions concerned with teaching. Of course, this does not mean that stress resulting from any of the life events should be overlooked. Certainly, teachers as well as others are subjected to both desirable and undesirable stress in situations not related to the job. However, the main focus of this book is to take into account those stressful conditions which are most relevant to the profession of teaching. To this end, the remainder of the book will be devoted primarily to these conditions with suggestions as to what action one might take in dealing with them.

CHAPTER 4

STRESS MANAGEMENT FOR TEACHERS

Stress management is concerned with a *lifestyle* that enable a person to deal with, and insofar as possible, avoid undesirable stress. To begin with, one should conduct his or her lifestyle with the application of certain basic principles. Obviously, there are no resolute standard procedures that are guaranteed to relieve a person entirely from undesirable stress. There are, however, certain general principles that may be applied to help alleviate stressful conditions.

All life pursuits involve both general and specific factors. In the case of dealing with stress, there are certain general principles that are likely to apply to most individuals. On the other hand, there are certain specific procedures for *coping* with stress that may be used by an individual according to how these procedures might meet his or her particular need. Subsequent chapters will deal with more or less specific techniques for coping with stress. The present discussion is concerned with some general principles of dealing with stress which in one way or another can be applied to practically all teachers.

We interpret the term *principle* to mean *guide to action.* Thus, the following general principles for dealing with stress should be considered as guidelines, but not necessarily in any particular order of importance. Moreover, it should be recognized that each principle is not a separate entity unto itself. This means that all of the principles are in some way interrelated and interdependent.

Personal health practices should be carefully observed. This is an easy principle to accept but sometimes it is difficult to implement. No one is against health, but not everyone abides by those practices that can help to maintain a suitable level of health. Teachers with their imposing schedules may be prone to neglect the basic requirements

49

that are essential for the human organism to reach an adequate functional level. Disregard for such important needs as proper diet, adequate rest and sleep, sufficient physical activity, and balancing work with play can reduce one's ability to deal with the stressful conditions inherent in the job of teaching.

These factors are not always neglected because teachers fail to recognize their importance. On the contrary, teachers, as well as many others may be lacking in knowledge with regard to certain health practices. In this connection, subsequent discussions in this chapter are intended to provide useful information.

There should be continuous self-evaluation. The practice of constantly taking stock of one's activities can help to minimize problems encountered on the job of teaching. This can be accomplished in part by taking a little time at the end of each day for an evaluation of the events that occurred during the day and one's reactions to those events. Setting aside this time period to review performance in the classroom is not only important to the achievement of goals but it is also important for remaining objective. Teachers will more likely be able to identify certain problems over which they have no control, and thus they will try to make an adjustment until such time that a positive change can be affected.

Learn to recognize your own accomplishments. You must learn to recognize your own accomplishments and praise yourself for them, especially if such praise is not offered by others. This is generally known as "stroking," or "patting one's self on the back," so to speak. In practicing this procedure teachers can develop positive attitudes and/or belief systems about their own accomplishments and thus reduce stress.

Learn to take one thing at a time. This is concerned with time budgeting and procrastination. Some teachers are likely to put things off and as a consequence frustrations can build up as tasks pile up. There is a need to sort out those tasks in order of importance and attack them one at a time. Proper budgeting of time can help to alleviate procrastination which in itself can be a stress inducing factor. Budgeting of time can help to eliminate worries of time urgency and the feeling of "too much to do in too short a time."

Learn to take things less seriously. This should not be interpreted to mean that teaching should be taken any less seriously. It does mean that there can be a fine line between what is actually serious and what is not. Sometimes when people look back at a particular event, they may wonder how they could have become so excited about it. Those teachers who are able to see the humorous side in the classroom tend to look at a potentially stressful situation more objectively, and this can assist them in keeping stress levels low.

Do things for others. Teachers can sometimes take their mind off their own stressful conditions by offering to do something for another person—a student or colleague. When teachers are helpful to others in attempting to relieve them of stress, they in turn will tend to be relieved of stress themselves. Much research tends to show that those persons who volunteer to help others oftentimes get as much benefit from this practice as those they volunteer to help.

Talk things over with others. Teachers sometimes tend to keep things to themselves and thus they may not be aware that others may be disturbed by the same things. Sometimes discussing something with a colleague or with a spouse can help one see things in a much different light. It is important to keep in mind that such discussion, particularly with colleagues, should be positive and objective lest it degenerate into idle gossip. This, of course, can tend to cause deterioration of a situation that is already at a low ebb.

Stress should not be confused with challenge. Oftentimes teachers relate stress to producing tensions and therefore expect anxiety to result. On the contrary, constructive stress in the right amounts can challenge a teacher and promote motivation, thinking, and task completion. Thus, recognizing stress as a natural phenomenon of life is no doubt one of the first and most important steps in dealing with it.

Making application of the above principles as a part of one's lifestyle can go a long way in keeping undesirable stress at bay.

A LIFESTYLE CONCERNED
WITH PERSONAL HEALTH

There appear to be two general factors to consider with regard to stress and health. First, objective evidence continues to accumulate to support the idea that prolonged stressful conditions can be most detrimental to the health of some individuals. And, second along with new and modern techniques of relieving stress, are many traditional health practices that long have helped people gain better control of their lives and thus reduce the negative effects of stressful living. It is our primary function here to deal with the second factor in the hope that the discussions will have a positive impact upon eliminating, or at least minimizing the conditions concerned with the first fractor. To this end subsequent discussions in this chapter will deal with what we will call the *fitness triangle:* (a) nutrition, (b) physical activity and exercise, and (c) rest and sleep. Before getting into specific discussions on these various areas, it seems appropriate to give some consideration to the general area of health.

The Meaning of Health

The precise meaning that one associates with the term health depends in a large measure upon the particular frame of reference in which it is used. In past years it was a relatively common practice to think of health in terms of the condition of a living organism that is functioning normally. This idea about health is one that is still accepted by many people. In subscribing to this particular concept these individuals tend to think of health predominantly as a state in which there is absence of pain or symptoms related to a poorly functioning organism. When thought of only in this manner, health is considered primarily in terms of a state in which there is absence of disease.

In modern times health is being considered more and more in terms of *well-being,* which is perhaps our most important human value. In considering health from a point of view of well-being, the ideal state of health would perhaps be one in which all of the various parts of the human organism function at an optimum level at all times. Although it is very unlikely that the human organism will ever achieve the ideal state suggested here, such a level is ordinarily used as a standard for diagnosing or appraising the human health status.

The old meaning of health that considered it primarily only in terms of absence of disease tended to place it in a *negative* sense. The more modern concept places more *positive* emphasis on the term. This is to say that the meaning of health is interpreted as a level of well-being also. It seems logical to assume that modern society's goal should be directed toward achieving the highest level of well-being for all of its citizens.

Health Knowledge, Attitudes and Practice

Any discussion of health should consider the three important aspects of health knowledge, health attitudes, and health practices. Each of these dimensions will be dealt with separately in the ensuing discussion, but it appears important at the outset to consider them together for the purpose of a better understanding of how they are related.

In order to benefit from health learning experiences, it is most important that these experiences develop into desirable health practices. Thus, the ultimate goal should be in the direction of a kind of behavior that is likely to insure optimum present and future health for the individual. However, before the most desirable and worthwhile health practices can be achieved, there is a need for a certain amount of desirable health knowledge along with a proper attitude in applying this knowledge to health practice.

Although it is obvious that *to know* is not necessarily *to do;* nevertheless, that which is done wisely will depend in a large measure upon the kind and amount of knowledge one has acquired. In the accumulation of health knowledge one will need to understand *why* it is beneficial to follow a certain practice. When one knows why, it is perhaps more likely that he or she will develop a desirable attitude toward certain health practices. If a person has developed a sufficient amount of desirable health knowledge through valid health concepts, and also has a proper attitude, then he or she will be more apt to apply the knowledge in health behavior. Morever, one should be in a better position to exercise good judgment and make wise decisions in matters pertaining to health if the right kind and amount of health knowledge has been obtained.

Health Knowledge. A somewhat frightening lack of knowledge about health was revealed recently in a national health test. In a nationwide sampling, 46 percent of the population had a score of poor; 27 percent, fair; 14 percent, good; and 13 percent, excellent. Among other things, this test indicated that only a very small percentage of the population could identify even three of the seven early possible signs of cancer. This is certainly not a very encouraging situation in a nation that is considered to have some of the foremost educational facilities in the world.

Knowledge about health is acquired in a variety of different ways. Some of it is the product of tradition, and, as such, is oftentimes nothing more than folklore. Certain popular notions about health-related matters that have long since been dispelled by the scientific community are still held by many people who have not, for some reason or other, benefited from modern health knowledge.

Other kinds of health knowledge of sorts are derived in our modern society from the constant bombardment of the eyes and ears by mass communication media such as television and radio. Although some of this information may be valid from a health point of view, everyone should be aware that the primary purpose of many kinds of advertising is to sell a product, and that in consequence they claim results that are not always likely to be attainable.

Another source of health knowledge is the home. In fact, most of our important health knowledge gets its start in the home. Parents are our first teachers and, for better or for worse, what we learn from them, mostly without our being aware that we are learning it, tends to remain with us. A good home should contribute much to the health knowledge of its children simply by providing good meals, and a friendly, well-regulated, but pleasant and recreationally challenging environment in which to grow up. Children from such homes ordinarily do not have to *unlearn* a lot of faulty ideas and unwholesome attitudes when they arrive at the next great potential source of health knowledge—the schools. It should be borne in mind that many children who grow up in homes in the inner city and some remote parts of the country do not benefit from good home experiences and thus their first source of health knowledge is the school. Possibly some of you as teachers have certain responsibilities for providing various kinds of health learning experiences for students within the framework of the school curriculum.

The scope of knowledge that one might obtain about matters related to health is almost endless, and obviously it would be well nigh impossible to learn all there is to know about it. However, there are certain basic concepts about health that should be developed by individuals at all age levels. Generally speaking, the individual should acquire knowledge pertaining to the direct basic needs of the organism, and, in addition, knowledge regarding the human organism as it functions in its environment.

Health Attitudes. Any discussion of attitudes requires an identification of the meaning of the term. Although it is recognized that different people will attach different meanings to the term attitude, for our purposes we would like to think of attitude as being associated with *feelings.* We hear such expressions as "How do you *feel* about it?" In a sense, this implies, "What is your *attitude* toward it?" Therefore, theoretically at least, attitude could be considered a factor in the determination of action because of this feeling about something. For example, knowledge alone that exercise is beneficial will not necessarily lead to regular exercising, but a strong feeling or attitude might be a determining factor that leads one to exercise regularly.

It should be mentioned at this point that, contrary to abundant empirical thought, there is little or no objective evidence to support unequivocally the contention that attitude has a positive direct influence on behavior. One of the difficulties in studying this phenomenon scientifically lies in the questionable validity of instruments used to measure attitude. Moreover, there is no consistent agreement with regard to the meaning of attitudes. Thus, the position taken here is one of theoretical postulation based upon logical assumption.

As far as health attitudes are concerned, they might be viewed as a gap that can exist between health knowledge and health practice, and this gap needs to be bridged if effective health behavior is to result from acquiring valid health knowledge. Let us consider as an example a teacher who has acquired some knowledge regarding the degree to which cigarette smoking can be harmful to health. Perhaps the teacher will have some sort of underlying feeling toward such knowledge. The teacher may choose to disregard it because some friends have also assumed such an attitude toward it, or the teacher may feel that the evidence is convincing enough to believe that cigarette smoking is something that one can get along without. In either case, the teacher has developed an attitude toward the practice of cigarette smoking and may act in accordance with this feeling. It should also be mentioned that the teacher may not necessarily react in accordance with his or her true feelings because he or she considers it fashionable to smoke cigarettes so as not to lose status with friends who do. Whichever way the teacher chooses to react will be tempered at least to an extent by the consequences that are associated with the knowledge acquired about cigarette smoking.

Obviously, one would hope that the accumulation of health knowledge would be accompanied by a positive attitude, and that this attitude would result in desirable action. It is possible that only in terms of such a positive attitude are desirable health practices, and thus, a better way of living, likely to result.

Health Practice. It was suggested previously that *to know* is not necessarily *to do.* It is a well-known fact that all people do not capitalize on the knowledge they have acquired. Perhaps many are apt to act only on impulse; actions of others are influenced to an extent by their friends. However, in a matter as important as one's health, it appears reasonable to follow a course where the individual weighs the facts and scientific evidence before acting.

Perhaps one might look at health practices that are desirable and those that are undesirable, or, in other words, those health practices that will result in pleasantness or unpleasantness. If one weighs knowledge in these terms, then perhaps one can appreciate better the possible consequences of certain health practices.

To change behavior is not always an easy matter. However, we hope that most persons will want to make a positive modification of their own health behavior after

acquiring health knowledge and forming favorable attitudes. In the final analysis the individual will make the decisions regarding his or her own health practices.

Daniel Boone once remarked that "profit is born of
risk." In modern society the converse might be true in
terms of the risks that people tend to take in matters pertaining to health. As far as one's personal health is concerned, it perhaps becomes a matter of how much risk one
is willing to take, and one's health practices are likely to be
based on this factor. By way of illustration we will refer
again to cigarette smoking and health. To our knowledge,
it has never been demonstrated scientifically that cigarette
smoking is in any way beneficial to the physical health of
the human organism; on the contrary, there has been a
great deal of information accepted as evidence from a
medical point of view that indicates that smoking can contribute to certain types of serious diseases. Yet untold
numbers of people are willing to assume a dangerous risk
in defiance of such evidence. After a person has learned
about some aspect of health, he or she is left with an ele-
ment of choice. We would hope to see a course of health
action chosen that will involve a minimum of risk.

A LIFESTYLE CONCERNED WITH
THE FITNESS TRIANGLE

In the final analysis there are three basic essentials needed to maintain the human organism at a reasonable level of
health. These are intake and utilization of proper foods,
sufficient physical activity and exercise, and adequate rest
and sleep. We have labeled this triad the *Fitness Triangle*
and the following discussions will focus on how these factors can assist teachers in keeping undesirable stress under
control.

Nutrition

Nutrition can be described as the sum of the processes by which a person takes in and utilizes food substances; that is, the nourishment of the body by food. These processes consist of (a) ingestion, (b) digestion, (c) absorption, and (d) assimilation.

Ingestion derives from the Latin word *ingestum*, the past participle of *ingerere*, meaning "to take in," and in this context it means taking in food, or the act of eating. The process of *digestion* involves the breaking down or conversion of food into substances that can be *absorbed* through the lining of the intestinal tract and into the blood and used in the body. *Assimilation* is concerned with the incorporation or conversion of nutrients into protoplasm which is the essential material making up living cells.

The body needs nutrients or foods to keep it functioning properly. These nutrients fall into the broad groups of proteins, carbohydrates, fats, vitamins and minerals. (Although water is not a nutrient in the strictest sense of the word, it must be included, for nutrition cannot take place without it).

Three major functions of nutrients are: (a) building and repair of all body tissues, (b) regulation of all body functions, and (c) providing fuel for the body's energy needs. Although all of the nutrients can do their best work when they are in combination with other nutrients, each still has its own vital role to play.

Diet is an all-inclusive term used to refer to foods and liquids regularly consumed. The question is often raised, "What constitutes a balanced diet?" Essentially one answer is that along with sufficient fluids, one should include foods from the four basic food groups. These are the dairy group, the meat group, the vegetable and fruit group, and the bread and cereal group.

A guide to a balanced diet has been prepared by the staff of the United States Senate Select Committee on Nutrition and Human Needs. This Committee spent a great deal of time on hearings and research and some of its recommendations are listed as follows:

1. Eat less meat and more fish and poultry.
2. Replace whole milk with skim milk.
3. Reduce intake of eggs, butter and other high-cholesterol sources.
4. Cut back on sugars to 15 percent of daily caloric intake.
5. Reduce intake of salt to a total of three grams per day.
6. Eat more fruit, vegetables, and whole grains.

The above recommendations are directed to the general population. However, one important fact must be remembered, and this is that eating is an individual matter. The problem may not be so much one of following an arbitrary diet as of learning to know what foods and proportions of foods keep one functioning best. The body is capable of compensating for an imbalance in the nutrients that one fails to get if the shortage is made up within a reasonable period of time. In other words, it is not necessary to have an exactly balanced diet at every meal. Indeed, it is possible to miss meals—even to go for several days without food—and show no signs of malnutrition. The important consideration seems to be in the quality of the total intake over periods of time.

The foregoing observations should not be interpreted to mean that one should be indifferent or careless about food choices. In a sense, after all, you are what you eat. And, it is absurd that some people are more careful about what they feed their pets than they are about what they feed themselves. This kind of thoughtlessness has given rise to the claim that Americans are at once the most overfed and yet malnourished people in the world. Any radical departure from one's diet should be made only under the guidance of a physician and/or a qualified nutritionist.

We have said that you are what you eat. This old adage has recently been brought more clearly into focus because researchers now know that our bodies synthesize food substances known as *neurotransmitters*. Prominent nutritionists tend to be of the opinion that these neurotransmitters relay messages to the brain which, in turn, affects our moods, sex drive, appetite, and even personality. This is to say that adding a certain food or omitting another could be just what a person might need. It is believed that when a person is stressed the body becomes less able to make use of protein. Therefore, the general recommendation is that after any kind of stress one should eat more lean meat, fish, or milk products. Also, since stress depletes the supply of vitamin C and potassium, these should be replaced by eating extra portions of citrus products.

Diet and Weight Control. The previously mentioned study found that "keeping an eye on weight" was a major concern of many teachers. In addition, "overweight" was identified as a major health problem among teachers.

Basically, weight gain or loss is a matter of energy intake versus energy expenditure of the body. If one wishes to decrease body fat one can reduce caloric intake (which is most easily done by reducing the amount of high-energy foods) and increase energy expenditure (by means of physical activity). By doing both, one can lower the weight a given amount in a given time by less severe dieting than would otherwise be necessary to accomplish the same thing. Some authorities feel that it may be a mistake to make reducing a matter of "will power." As in trying to stop smoking, will power may set up a desperate struggle from which the habit is likely to emerge victorious. Or a substitute habit may be acquired, as in the case of the man who gave up drinking altogether—and has since been a helplessly obsessive gambler. The wiser course might be to determine why eating has become of disproportionate importance in life and, as in the case cited earlier, discover what needs to be done about it.

Because dieting is the most popular way of controlling weight it seems appropriate to establish general principles when one undertakes the practice. The following list of such principles might well be considered by anyone contemplating a weight control program.

1. Seek the advise of a physician and/or qualified nutritionist.
2. If fat is to be lost, the calories taken in must be fewer than those needed for the body's energy requirements.
3. The diet, though low in calories, must be adequate in all other nutrients so that intakes for these do not become dangerously low.
4. It should be recognized that losing weight is not easy.
5. Foods are not forbidden, but portion control is emphasized.
6. There should be a sensible balance of energy-providing nutrients.
7. The diet should be realistic and should not call for superhuman effort.
8. Exercise at the same time is recommended.
9. The behaviors and emotions that lead to eating should be examined, and advise sought to help the dieter control these.

Diet and Stress.   With very few exceptions, writers on the subject of stress emphasize the importance of diet as a general health measure. However, the question to pose is: "Are there any specific forms of diet that can contribute to the prevention of stress and/or help one cope with it?" (We have already mentioned how some foods might be used when one is under stress, and later we will comment on the controversy surrounding the use of the so-called "stress formula vitamins").

One specific approach to diet and stress is presented by Dr. J. Daniel Palm, who suggests that many stress-initiated disorders are related to problems that originate in the regulation of the blood sugar level. (61)

Dr. Palm's theory, developed as an extension of the data derived from controlled research, states that an insufficiency of sugar in the blood supplied to the brain is enough of a detrimental condition, and therefore a stress, to initiate physiological responses and behavioral changes that develop into a variety of disorders. A deficiency of blood sugar which is known to be associated with a variety of disorders is seen not as a consequence of the disease but as a primary and original physiological stress. Behavioral changes may represent inadequate or inappropriate attempts of the stresss-affected persons to compensate. It is believed that if stress from an insufficiency of blood sugar can be prevented, various kinds of abnormal behavior can be controlled. To eliminate this stress of a deficiency of blood sugar a new dietary program is proposed by Dr. Palm. This diet is based on the metabolic characteristics of *fructose* (fruit sugar) and its advantageous use when it is exchanged for glucose or other carbohydrates which are digested to glucose and then absorbed. (Fructose itself is a normal constituent of sucrose, which is ordinary table sugar. It also occurs naturally in many fruits and constitutes half the content of honey).

Practically all theories have enthusiastic proponents as well as equally unenthusiastic opponents, and this sometimes results in a great deal of confusion among many people. The fact that the human organism is so complicated and complex makes any kind of research connected with it extremely difficult. Nevertheless, scholars in the scientific community continue to make important inquiries into the study of human needs.

Vitamins and Stress. From a historical point of view, the realization that vitamins are basic nutrients stands as a milestone in the emergence of the field of nutrition as a scientifically based discipline. Unlike such nutrients as protein, fats, and minerals, vitamins do not become a part of the structure of the body, but rather they serve as catalysts that make possible various chemical reactions within the body. These reactions have to do with converting food substances into the elements needed for utilization by the various cells of the body. For example, vitamin D needs to be present if calcium is to be metabolized and made available for use in the blood and bones.

The vitamins with which we are familiar today are commonly classified as *fat*-soluble and *water*-soluble. This designation means that the one group requires fatty substances and the other water if they are to be dissolved and used by the body. Although a large number of vitamins have been identified as being important to human nutrition, the exact function of some of them has not yet been determined.

In countries such as the United States it should not be difficult for people to select a diet that is sufficiently varied to include all necessary vitamins. However, poor dietary practices can lead to vitamin inadequacy, and as a precaution many people supplement their diets with vitamin pills. Even though such a supplement may not be needed, when taken in small amounts the vitamins may do no harm. This is particularly true of the water-soluble vitamins in that if one gets more than is necessary, they will pass right through the body. (Recently, some scientists have been disputing this claim, especially if water-soluble vitamins are taken in extra large doses). On the other hand, some of the fat-soluble vitamins may be toxic and overdoses could render possible harm. Of course, extra vitamins may be prescribed by physicians for a variety of reasons ranging from suspected malnutrition, to pregnancy, chronic fatigue, and postsurgical recovery.

In recent years a great deal of controversy has emerged as a result of what has been called *megavitamin therapy,* which concerns the use of certain vitamins in massive doses—sometimes as much as 1,000 times the U. S. Recommended Daily Allowances. The proponents for megavitamin therapy believe that massive doses of such vitamins, particularly vitamin C, and in some cases the B-complex vitamins, will prevent certain diseases and very significantly extend life. On the contrary, opponents of the practice maintain that it not only may be useless, but in some instances harmful as well.

It is interesting to note that there is some support for massive dosages of certain vitamins as an important factor in surviving stress. In fact, there is a special class of vitamins sold over the counter called *stress formula vitamins.* The formula for these is one that includes large amounts of vitamin C and vitamin B-complex.

Anyone contemplating utilizing a vitamin supplement over and above the U. S. Recommended Daily Allowances should do so in consultation with a physician and/or qualified nutritionist.

Physical Activity and Exercise

When used in connection with the human organism the term *physical* means a concern for the body and its needs. The term *activity* derives from the word *active,* one meaning of which is the requirement of action. Thus, when the two words physical and activity are used together it implies body action. This is a broad term and could include any voluntary and/or involuntary body movement. When such body movement is practiced for the purpose of developing and maintaining physical fitness, it is ordinarily referred to as physical *exercise.* This section of the chapter is concerned with both the broad area of physical activity and the more specific area of physical exercise as they relate to stress.

The answer to the question, "Why exercise?" is relatively simple. Wherever there is muscle there is a need for movement. The human body contains more than 600 muscles; overall, it is more than half muscle. Muscles make possible every overt motion. They also push food along the digestive tract, suck air into the lungs, and tighten blood vessels to raise blood pressure when more pressure is needed to meet an emergency. The heart itself is a muscular pump. Muscles are meant to be used and when they are not used, or not used enough, they can deteriorate. If one is habitually inactive and succumbs to the philosophy of easy living—he or she must then pay the price in decreased efficiency.

Importance of Physical Exercise in Coping with Stress. The value of exercise as a means of coping with stress is well documented by authoritative sources. For example, Dr. Beata Jencks reports that physical and emotional trauma upset the balance of body and mind, so that much energy is wasted in muscular tension, bringing on unnecessay tiredness and exhaustion. If stress reactions become habit patterns, the muscles and tendons shorten and thicken, and excessive connective tissue is deposited, causing a general consolidation of tissues. She comments further that excess energy, released by action of the sympathetic nervous system, if not immediately dissipated by muscular action, produces muscular or nervous tension, and this tension may then be dissipated by muscular action in the form of exercise. (38)

Recently it has been theorized that exercise will boost the level of *beta-endorphins,* the natural opium-like substances produced by the body. The endorphins in turn are supposed to reduce anxiety and give a person a good feeling. However, research in this area has shown inconsistent results. Incidentally, a forthcoming selection in this series on Stress in Modern Society by Drs. Bonnie G. Berger and Bradly D. Hatfield will present a detailed, authoritative account on *Exercise and Stress.*

Basic Factors in Physical Fitness. In an oversimplified but useful way, physical fitness can be reduced to (a) strength and (b) endurance. For purposes of the present discussion we shall assume a good diet, adequate rest and sleep, and other good health practices.

Strength, which is the ability to mobilize force to overcome resistance, has to do with the ability of muscle fibers to contract, and it is determined on the basis of how much weight a contraction of one's muscle fiber can move or support. Strength is required for all forms of muscular work, whether it be milking a cow, writing, or picking up weight. Strength may be considered "adequate" if one can lift everything one needs or wishes to lift, without undue strain. Life is a lot simpler if one can do lifting effortlessly—which is to say one's reserve strength is well above ordinary weight-moving requirements.

Generally speaking, muscle size is related to strength. This is, if one wants to build up muscles for appearance's sake, or for any other reason, there is a need to engage in strength-building activities. This means that employment of the "overload" principle, the essence of which is to keep requiring a little more of a group of muscles than it can easily do. If the weight or resistance is gradually increased over a period of time, one can do easily what one used to be able to do only with great effort or not at all, and the muscles will tend to increase proportionately.

Two types of strength are *isometric* strength and *isotonic* strength. Isometric strength, sometimes referred to as *static* strength, involves the maximal amount of force that can be applied against a fixed resistance during one all-out effort. An example of this would be pushing or pulling against an immovable object. Isotonic strength, sometimes referred to as *dynamic* strength, involves the amount of resistance one can overcome during one application of force through the full range of motion of a given joint or joints. An example of this would be picking up a weight with both hands and flexing the elbows while lifting the weight, let us say to shoulder level.

Although for the most part, men may exercise for the purpose of building up large muscles, such is not necessarily the case for women. Although many women exercise in order to build up or maintain their strength, they are obviously not as interested as men in developing large muscles. Their exercises are usually less strenuous and emphasize endurance activities over strength-building ones. We shall discuss endurance later; however, we should like to emphasize in passing that having good, strong, useful muscles does not make a woman "masculine" in appearance or otherwise. Outstanding women gymnasts and swimmers, for example, whose muscles have been well developed, are frequently not only "well built" but attractively so in the feminine sense. That is, physical fitness enhances attractiveness. Physical weakness is not a guarantee of femininity for women, but it can be a guarantee of easy fatigue and an inability to enjoy some of the good things that life has to offer.

Whereas strength is concerned with the amount of work that muscle fibers can accomplish in a single contraction, *endurance* has to do with how long the fibers can continue to contract. All endurance activities also involve strength to one degree or another. For example, little strength, but considerable endurance, would be required to lift a small weight overhead many times.

Although muscular endurance is an important factor in doing repetitious work, especially of short duration, the major consideration in most prolonged bodily activity is circulatory fitness. That is, endurance in activities like running for distance is dependent upon the efficiency with which the heart and lungs make oxygen available to the working muscles and with which fatigue products are disposed of. (Activities of this nature are now commonly being referred to as *aerobic* activities).

Developing Your Own Program.   The initial step before embarking on a physical activity program is to get a complete medical examination. It is likely that one's physician will recommend the program without restriction, or if a physical problem is found, steps can be taken to correct it—and the physician may have suggestions for modifying the program to make it more suitable. However, after an examination it is likely that one can proceed with confidence.

The next consideration is that the program be an individual matter and one that fits your own needs and wishes. In other words, if you are not happy with the program it is unlikely to meet with success as far as your personal goals are concerned. Each individual will have to determine which particular approach is best, specified physical exercises, recreational sports, or a combination of both. When you decide that you want to change from a more or less sedentary existence to a more active one, there are certain steps involved in such a change. In their excellent best seller *Total Fitness in Thirty Minutes a Week*, Dr. Laurence E. Morehouse and Leonard Gross suggest the following three steps involved in such a change. (54)

1. The first step is simply to accept the importance and necessity of physical activity. You know you can always find time to do the things you really want to do.

2. The second step is to schedule the activity in spite of everything else you have to do. It then becomes one of the high-priority items of your day or week.

3. The third and probably the most difficult step is to work on your attitude toward exercise

Obviously, space does not permit us to include in detail all of the various possibilities for physicial activity programs. There are many fine sources of such information, one of which is available for a small charge from the U.S. Government Printing Office in Washington, D.C., entitled *Adult Physical Fitness*. We do, however, wish to concentrate our attention on some activities that can have immediate application when stressful conditions arise in the classroom.

Instant Physical Activities for Coping with Stress in the Classroom.   It has been mentioned on several occasions in the book that there are many stress inducing factors in the school situation, and a number of these occur right in the classroom. A part of the foregoing discussion in the present chapter has focused on the importance of physical activity in helping one cope with stress. The present discussion is concerned with a teacher's active behavior in a stressful classroom situation. More specifically, what can a teacher do in the way of physical activity to copy with a stressful situation in the classroom?

Various authentic pronouncements have been made which support the idea that such activity can be beneficial. For example, Drs. Reuven Gal and Richard S. Lazarus report that being engaged in activity—rather than remaining passive—is preferable for most individuals in most stressful situations and can be highly effective in reducing threat and distress. (30) Morever, the latter has maintained that a person may alter his or her psychological and physiological stress reactions in a given situation simply by taking action, and this in turn will affect his or her appraisal of the situation thereby uttimately altering the stress reaction. (42)

What then are some of the physical activities that a teacher can engage in as reactions to a stressful situation in the classroom? Obviously, it would not be appropriate to drop to the floor and start doing push-ups, or to break into a two-mile jog around the room. The activities that we are recommending for this purpose can be performed in a more or less subtle manner and not even be noticed by students or other observers. (It is a well-known fact that outside observers such as the principal can put some teachers under stress the moment they enter the room). The following are some possibilities, and certainly the creative teacher will be able to think of numerous others.

1. *Hand and Head Press.* Interweave fingers and place hands at the back of the head with elbows pointing out. Push the head backward on the hands while simultaneously pulling the head forward with the hands. Although this can be done while standing, it can also be done while sitting at the desk and is then less conspicuous.

2. *Wall Press.* Stand with the bank against the wall. Allow the arms to hand downward at the sides. Turn hands toward the wall and press the wall with the palms, keeping the arms straight.

3. *Hand Pull.* Bend the right elbow and bring the right hand palm up close to the front of the body. Put the left

hand in the right hand. Try to curl the right arm upward while simultaneously resisting with the left hand. Repeat, using opposite pressure. This can be done while standing or sitting at the desk.

4. *Hand Push.* The hands are clasped with the palms together close to the chest with the elbows pointing out. Press the hands together firmly. This can be done while standing or sitting at the desk.

5. *Leg Press.* While sitting at the desk, cross the left ankle over the right ankle. The feet are on the floor and the legs are at about a right angle. Try to straighten the right leg while resisting with the left leg. Repeat, with the right ankle over the left ankle.

6. *The Gripper.* Place one hand in the other hand and grip hard. This can be done while standing or sitting at the desk. Another variation is to grip an object. While standing, this could be the back of a chair, or while sitting it could be the arms of a chair, or the seat.

7. *Chair Push.* While sitting at the desk with the hands on the armrest of the chair, push down with the hands. The entire buttocks can be raised from the chair seat. One or both feet can be lifted off the floor, or both can remain in contact with the floor.

8. *Hip Lifter.* While sitting at the desk, lift one buttock after the other from the chair seat. Try to keep the head from moving. The hands can be placed at the sides of the chair seat for balance.

9. *Heal and Toe.* From a standing position, rise on the toes. Come back down on the heels while raising both the toes and the balls of the feet.

10. *Fist Clencher.* Clench the fist and then open the hands extending the fingers as far as possible.

This short list is comprised of representative examples of push and pull (isometric) exercises, and they are actually referred to be some people as *stress* exercises. Although we have recommended these as types of activities that can be performed easily in the classroom, it is obvious that, along with others, they can be performed elsewhere as well. Wherever isometric exercises are performed it might be well to observe the following recommendations of the President's Council on Physical Fitness:

One hard six to eight-second isometric contraction per workout can, over a period of six months, produce a significant strength increase in a muscle. There is no set order for doing them—nor does a whole series have to be completed at one time. For each contaction, maintain tension for *no more than eight seconds.* Do little breathing during the contraction; breathe deeply between contractions. Start easily, and do *not* apply maximum effort in the beginning. For the first three or four weeks, you should exert only about one-half of what you think is your maximum force. Use the first three or four seconds to build up to this degree of force—and the remaining four or five seconds to hold it. (1)

Rest and Sleep

To be effective in the job of teaching and to enjoy leisure to the utmost, periodic recuperation is an essential ingredient in daily living patterns. Rest and sleep provide us with the means of revitalizing ourselves to meet the challenges of our responsibilities.

In order to keep fatigue at a minimum and in its proper proportion in the cycle of everyday activities, nature has provided ways that help to combat and reduce it. First, however, we should consider what fatigue is so that it may then be easier to cope with it.

There are two types of fatigue, *acute* and *chronic.* Acute fatigue is a natural outcome of sustained or severe exertion. It is due to such physical factors as the accumulation of the by-products of muscular exertion in the blood and excessive "oxygen debt"—that is, the inability of the body to take in as much oxygen as is being consumed by muscu-

lar work. Psychological considerations may also be important in acute fatigue. That is, an individual who becomes
bored with his work and who becomes preoccupied with
the discomfort involved will become "fatigued" much
sooner than if he is highly motivated to do the same work,
is not bored, and does not think about the discomfort.

Activity that brings on distressing acute fatigue in one
individual may amount to mild, even pleasant, exertion to
another. The difference in fatigue level is due essentially
to the physical fitness, that is, training, of the individual for
the particular work under consideration. Thus, a good
walker or dancer may soon become fatigued when running
or swimming hard. The key, then, to controlling acute fatigue is sufficient training in the activities to be engaged in
to prevent premature and undue fatigue. Knowing one's
limits at any given time is also important as a guide to
avoiding excessively fatiguing exertion and to determining
that preparatory training is necessary.

Chronic fatigue has reference to fatigue that lasts over
extended periods—in contract with acute fatigue that
tends to be followed by a recovery period and restoration
to "normal" within a more or less brief period of time.
Chronic fatigue may be due to any of a variety of medical
conditions ranging from a disease to malnutrition. (Such
conditions are the concern of the physician who, incidentally, should evaluate all cases of chronic fatigue so as to as-
sure that a disease condition is not responsible). It may also
be due to psychological factors such as extreme boredom
and/or worry about having to do, over an extended period,
what one does not wish to do.

Activity is essential to life, but so are rest and sleep, as
they afford the body the chance to regain its vitality and efficiency in a very positive way. Learning to utilize oppor-
tunities for rest and sleep may add years to our lives and
zest to our years. Although rest and sleep are closely al-
lied, they are not synonymous. For this reason it seems appropriate to consider them separately.

In general, most people think of *rest* as just "taking it easy." A chief purpose of rest is to reduce tension so that the body may be better able to recover from fatigue. There is no overt activity involved, but neither is there loss of consciousness as in sleep. In rest there is no loss of awareness of the external environment as in sleep. Since the need for sleep is usually in direct proportion to the type of activity in which we engage, it follows naturally that the more strenuous the activity, the more frequent the rest periods should be. A busy day at school may not be as noticably active as a game of tennis; nevertheless, it is the wise teacher who will let the body dictate when a rest period is required. Five or ten minutes of sitting in a chair with eyes closed may make the difference in the course of an active school day, assuming of course that this is possible. The real effectiveness of rest periods depends largely on the individual and his or her ability to let down and rest.

Sleep is a phenomenon that has never been clearly defined or understood but has aptly been named the "great restorer." An old Welsh proverb states that "disease and sleep are far apart." It is no wonder that authorities on the subject agree that sleep is essential to the vital functioning of the body and that natural sleep is the most satisfying form of recuperation from fatigue. It is during the hours of sleep that the body is given an opportunity to revitalize itself. All vital functions are slowed down so that the building of new cells and the repair of tissues can take place without undue interruption. This does not mean that the body builds and regenerates tissue only during sleep, but it does mean that it is the time that nature has set aside to accomplish the task more easily. The body's metabolic rate is lowered, some waste products are eliminated, and energy is restored.

Despite the acknowledged need for sleep, a question of paramount importance concerns the amount of sleep necessary for the body to accomplish its recuperative task. There is no clear-cut answer to this query. Sleep is an individual matter based on degree rather than kind. The usual recommendation for adults is eight hours of sleep out of every 24, but the basis for this could well be fallacy rather than fact. There are many persons who can function effectively on much less sleep while others require more. No matter how many hours of sleep one gets during the course of a 24-hour period the real test of adequacy will depend largely upon how one feels. If you are normally alert, feel healthy, and are in good humor, you are probably getting a sufficient amount of sleep. The rest that sleep normally brings to the body depends to a large extent upon a person's freedom from excessive emotional tension and ability to relax. Unrelaxed sleep has little restorative value, but learning to relax is a skill that is not acquired in one night. (Some recommendations in this connection will be made in the final chapter).

Is loss of sleep dangerous? This is a question that is pondered quite frequently. Again, the answer is not simple. To the normally healthy person with normal sleep habits an occasional missing of the accustomed hours of sleep is not serious. On the other hand, repeated loss of sleep over a period of time can be dangerous. It is the loss of sleep night after night rather than at one time that apparently does the damage and results in the condition previously described as chronic fatigue. The general effects of loss of sleep are likely to result in poor general health, nervousness, irritability, inability to concentrate, lowered perseverance of effort, and serious fatigue. Studies have shown that a person can go for much longer periods of time without food than without sleep. In some instances successive loss of sleep for long periods have proven fatal. Under normal conditions, however, a night of lost sleep followed by a period of prolonged sleep will restore the individual to his normal physiological self.

There are many conditions that tend to rob the body of restful slumber. Most certainly, mental tension and worry play a very large part in holding sleep at bay. Factors that influence the quality of sleep are hunger, cold, boredom, and excessive fatigue. In many instances these factors can be controlled. Incidentally, it is interesting to note that Dr. Robert Coursey, a psychologist at the University of Maryland and a researcher of sleep, has indicated that people who are "insomniacs" may only think they are, and one of the things that insomniacs worry about is their sleepless condition. His definition of a chronic insomniac is one who takes longer to fall asleep, has more trouble staying asleep, wakes up earlier than a normal sleeper and feels tired as a result. (16) In any case, insomnia and chronic fatigue might well be brought to the attention of a physician so that the necessary steps can be taken to bring about restoration of normal sleep patterns. And certainly, drugs to induce sleep should be utilized only if prescribed by a physician.

Many recommendations about sleep have been made by authoritative sources and some of these are cited here. One source suggests that techniques that will help are: (a) relaxing physically and mentally before retiring, (b) reducing your tension level during the day, and (c) managing your time, activities, and thoughts to prepare for a good night's sleep. (15) Another source recommends that the process should be the same each night, and should begin at the same hour, leading to repose at the same hour. That is, if your bedtime is normally eleven o'clock your preparation should begin at least by ten and not later than ten-thirty. If work has been brought home you should break off at least one-half hour before the fixed time of retirement. And during this half hour stimulants should be avoided, but a glass of warm milk can be an excellent tranquilizer. (55)

Understanding the complex nature of sleep may be the province of scientists and other qualified experts, but an understanding of the value of sleep is the responsibility of everyone.

The suggestions and recommendations made throughout this chapter have been intended to help teachers embark on and/or improve upon a lifestyle designed to eliminate undesirable stress—or at the very least to keep such stress levels at a low ebb.

CHAPTER 5

CONTROLLING TEACHER STRESS
THROUGH BEHAVIOR MODIFICATION

For purposes of this discussion we will consider *behavior* as anything that the organism does as a result of some sort of stimulation. A standard dictionary definition of the term *modification* is a "change in the organism caused by environmental factors." Thus, when the two terms are used together—behavior modification—they could be interpreted to mean some sort of change in the way a person has ordinarily reacted to a given stimulus.

Almost without exception, most descriptions of the term *learning* are characterized by the idea that learning involves some sort of change in the individual. This means that when an individual has learned, his behavior has changed in one or more ways. In this regard, it is significant that the *Dictionary of Education* defines *behavior modification* as a "change in the accustomed mode of behavior resulting from learning." (20)

In recent years behavior modification has become so broad in scope that it is used in many frames of reference. We would like to emphasize forcefully at this point that for our purposes we are *not* considering it as a variety of psychological and/or psychiatric techniques (patient-client relations) for altering behavior. On the contrary, our recommendations for the use of modification of behavior are confined to its possibilities as a means for teachers themselves to produce more effective teaching, and thus, helping to reduce certain stress-related factors involved in the teaching process. This is to say that if a teacher manifests a behavior that provokes a stressful situation, and further, if the teacher can change the behavior, it might be possible to eliminate or at least minimize the stressful condition. For example, let us say that a teacher constantly uses what students consider unwarranted criticism. This can create a

79

problem in teacher-student relations, and thus a stressful atmosphere.

Behavior modification in the whole area of education has been given increased attention in recent years. In fact, the National Society for the Study of Education devoted its entire 2nd Yearbook to this subject.

In general, the practice of behavior modification involves external assistance as in the case of a teacher trying to effect a behavior change in a student or a group of students. Our major concern here is in the direction of *self-modification*, with the teacher attempting to improve upon his or her own behavior. This assumes that the teacher generally can develop the ability to increase desirable or appropriate behavior and to decrease undesirable or inappropriate behavior. Of course, this involves *self-control* which can be described as, "manipulation of environmental events which influence one's own behavior for the purpose of changing the behavior." (23) Self-control can eventually lead to *behavioral self-management* which has been considered as the "learning and practicing of new habits." (15) Satisfactory self-control and successful behavioral self-management are obviously contingent upon some sort of understanding of *self*, the subject of the ensuing section of the chapter.

UNDERSTANDING YOURSELF

In order to put an understanding of self in its proper perspective, consideration needs to be given to the basic aspects of *self-structure* and *self-concept.* According to Dr. Hugh Perkins, (65) self-structure is the framework of a particular individual's complex of motives, perceptions, cognitions, feelings and values—the product of developmental processes. Self-structure is revealed in behavior. One reveals in his behavior the knowledge, skills, and interests he has acquired, the goals he is seeking, the beliefs, values, and attitudes he has adopted, the roles he has learned, and the self-concept he has formed. Thus, self-concept is an aspect of self-structure.

It is also suggested that among the most relevant and significant perceptions an individual acquires are those of himself in various life situations; and further, that the self-concept is basically made up of a large number of *percepts*, each of which contains one or more qualities that one ascribes to himself. To be more specific, *self-percept* pertains to sense impressions of a trait one ascribes to himself, while *self-concept* consists of the totality of one's self-percepts organized in some sort of order.

The frame of reference of self-concept with which we are concerned here involves the *total personality* concept. A great deal of clinical and experimental evidence indicates that a human being must be considered as a whole and not a collection of parts, and thus is a total personality.

But this immediately raises the question, "What comprises the total personality?" Anyone who has difficulty in formulating views with regard to what the human personality actually consists of can take courage in the knowledge that many experts who spend their time studying it are not always in complete agreement as to what it is or how it operates. However, if one were to analyze the literature on the subject it would be found generally agreed that the total personality consists of the sum of all the *physical, social, emotional*, and *intellectual* aspects of any individual. This can also be expressed in terms of the physical self, the social self, the emotional self, and the intellectual self, with everyone manifesting certain kinds of physical behavior, social behavior, emotional behavior, and intellectual behavior. Although this discussion deals with self-concept in a general way, as you read on you will no doubt want to try to visualize the way in which "your own self" corresponds to the general pattern. The importance of this approach is seen when you as an individual make an effort in the direction of self-modification of behavior.

The total personality is *one thing* comprising the above major aspects. All of these components are highly interrelated and interdependent. All are important to the balance and health of the personality because only in terms of their health can the personality as a whole maintain a completely healthy state. The condition of any one aspect affects each other aspect to a degree, and hence the personality as a whole.

When a nervous person stutters or becomes nauseated, it is not necessarily a mental state that is causing the physical symptom. On the contrary, a pressure imposed upon the organism causes a series of reactions, which includes thought, verbalization, digestive processes, and muscular function. Mind does not always cause the body to become upset; the *total* organism is upset by a situation, and reflects its upset in several ways, including disturbance in thought, feeling, and bodily processes. The whole individual responds in interaction with the social and physical environment. And, as the individual is affected by his environment, he in turn has an effect upon it.

Because of long tradition during which physical development *or* intellectual development, rather than physical *and* intellectual development, has been advocated, we oftentimes are still accustomed to dividing the two in our thinking. The result may be that we sometimes pull human beings apart with this kind of thinking. Traditional attitudes which separate mind and body tend to lead to unbalanced development of an individual with respect to mind and body and/or social adjustment.

It is interesting that in modern times, when great emphasis is placed upon social adjustment, faulty interpersonal relationships present such a major problem. For this reason it is important to make special note of the interaction between the individual and the environment. The quality of the individual's interpersonal relationships affect all other aspects of his personality. How well do you drive a car when someone is shouting at you? How well can you concentrate when you think someone is talking about you? These are social circumstances which affect the physical, emotional, and intellectual aspects of personality.

All of these things then are the basis of total personality—a complex balance of psychological and social considerations which prepare the individual for the fullest, most socially valuable, productive and adventuresome living. A large portion of the responsibility falls to the individual teacher to make those kinds of modifications in personal behavior that will in one way or another add to the quality of living and help in the prevention of undesirable stress.

SELF CONCERNS WHICH CAN INDUCE STRESS IN TEACHERS

Any discussion of *self* needs to include the important classification of stress-inducing factors that involve *personal* or *self* concerns. The following generalized descriptive list takes some of these factors into account.

1. *Self concerns associated with the meeting of personal goals.* Stress is likely to result if teachers set goals that are too difficult to accomplish. For example, teachers' goals may be much higher than a particular school environment will permit them to achieve. On the contrary, if teachers set goals that are too low, they may develop the feeling that they are not doing as much for students as they should. This aspect of stress is also concerned with the fear that some teachers have that they will not reach their goals in the teaching field. That is, they may believe that their talents could be put to better use in some other profession.

2. *Self concerns which involve self-esteem.* This involves the way one feels about oneself, and one's self-esteem can often be closely related to the fulfillment of certain *ego needs.* Some teachers may feel that there is not

enough status associated with the teaching profession. This may be more true in modern times than in times past, because in modern society in general the teaching profession is not held in the esteem that it enjoyed previously. It bothers some teachers too that their superiors do not praise them for what they consider to be a job well done. It is also stressful for young teachers who feel that they are not advancing as rapidly as they would like. Of course, this is a characteristic of many young people, regardless of their occupational pursuit.

3. *Self concerns related to changing values.* It is frustrating to some teachers if they feel that the value system in a given school environment does not meet their own standards. They may develop the feeling that students are not inclined to place a value on those factors which the teacher feels are important to their growth and development.

4. *Self concerns which center around social needs.* In some cases teachers feel that their own social life is neglected because of the demands for "outside" work that is associated with teaching. Such requirements as attending PTA meetings tend to infringe upon the social life that many teachers feel they deserve. Some teachers feel that not only is their own personal social life being neglected but that of their family as well.

5. *Self concerns involving personal competence and ability.* This is probably the self concern that frustrates teachers the most. Certainly, lack of confidence in one's ability can be devastating to the morale of a teacher. Teachers are becoming increasingly concerned with their ability, or lack thereof, to cope with such problems as: (a) providing for individual differences of students, (b) keeping up with the so-called "knowledge explosion," (c) participation in the sensitive teaching areas such as sex education and drug abuse, (d) an erosion of teaching ability because of the excessive demands made upon teachers, and (e) control in the classroom.

It should be mentioned that not all of these self concerns are characteristic of all teachers, particularly because of the individual differences among them. That is, what may be a serious self concern for one teacher may be a minimal concern for another.

PROCESSES OF BEHAVIORAL ADJUSTMENT

The term *adjustment* has been described as "the process of finding and adopting modes of behavior suitable to the environment or to changes in the environment." (20) In this regard, it seems appropriate to repeat one authority's definition of stress alluded to previously. That is, "environmental conditions that require *behavioral adjustment.*" (4)

Teaching involves a continuous sequence of experiences that are characterized by the necessity for the human organism to adjust. Consequently, it may be said that "normal" behavior is the result of successful adjustment, and abnormal behavior results from unsuccessful adjustment. The degree of adjustment which the individual achieves depends upon how adequately he is able to satisfy his basic needs and to fulfill his desires within the framework of his environment and the pattern or ways dictated by his society.

As mentioned previously, stress may be considered as any factor acting internally or externally which renders adaptation difficult, and which induces increased effort on the part of the person to maintain a state of equilibrium within himself and with his external environment. When stress is induced as a result of the person not being able to meet his needs (basic demands) and to satisfy his desires (wants or wishes), *frustration* or *conflict* results. Frustration results when a need is not met; and conflict results when (a) choices must be made between nearly equally attractive alternatives or (b) when basic emotional forces oppose one another. In the emotionally healthy individual the degree of frustration is ordinarily in proportion to the

intensity of the need or the desire. That is, he will objectively observe and evaluate the situation to ascertain
whether a solution is possible, and if so, what solution
would best enable him to achieve the fulfillment of needs
and desires. However, every person has a "zone of tolerance" or limits for physical, physiological, and psychological stress within which he normally operates. If the stress
becomes considerably greater than the tolerance level, or
if the individual has not learned to cope with his problems
and objectively and intelligently solve them, some degree
of maladjustment can result.

SOME GENERAL PROCEDURES FOR
SELF-MODIFICATION OF BEHAVIOR

Over the past several years a voluminous literature has
been published in the general area of behavior modification, and a portion of this material has been concerned
with behavior modification in education. Most of this has
been directed to school administrators, teachers, coun-
selors and others for the purpose of utilizing the procedure to produce behavior change in students. As mentioned previously, we are concerned here with *self*-
modification of behavior, and literature in this specific
area is becoming more abundant.

Although self-modification of behavior is considered a
relatively recent innovation, one report suggests that it
was used in the early history of our country by Benjamin
Franklin. (40) He is said to have used it to improve upon
such virtues as temperance and frugality. He kept a record
of the errors he thought he made each day in each of over a
dozen virtues. At the end of the day he would consult the
information to help him identify those virtues he may not
have been practicing. Of course, in modern times our approach to the self-modification of behavior is no doubt
much more sophisticated than that of Franklin, and improvement in procedures is constantly being made.

Whether an individual is attempting to modify the behavior of another (teacher with a student) or trying to modify his own behavior, the general procedures of application are essentially the same. There are certain sequential steps to be taken which include (a) identification and description of one's behaviors, (b) counting the behaviors, (c) attempting to effect a change in behaviors, and (d) evaluating the procedures used to change behaviors. The following discussion will take into account some of the important features involved in these various steps.

Identifying Behaviors

The first step in the process of self modification of behavior is concerned with identification of a behavior that one wishes to modify. This process is also referred to as *pinpointing, targeting,* or *specifying* a behavior. Essentially, this involves trying to define a particular behavior (target) which one wishes to change. This is not always an easy matter because sometimes a teacher may manifest a behavior that is annoying both to students and to others, but the teacher may be completely unaware of it.

When a teacher is able to identify a particular behavior and admit that such a behavior may be interfering with teaching effectiveness, a strong beginning can be made in the direction of a behavioral change. In other words, recognizing that one has a problem is the first prerequisite to solving it.

In many instances the identification of a behavior emerges when a teacher is dissatisfied with what he or she may be doing. For example, a teacher may find herself performing a behavior that she does not want to perform; or she may not be performing a behavior that she wants to perform.

Let us consider the hypothetical case of Ms. Pedagogue, a sixth-grade teacher who is enrolled in a night course in the "Psychology of Teaching" at a nearby university. In one class session on the general topic of "teacher attention," the discussion focused upon inappropriate teacher response to student behavior. It was brought out that one form of inappropriate behavior is the command given in response to a student behavior, for example, when there is a noise the teacher commands, "Be quiet!" Or, when students are out of their seats, the teacher commands, "Sit down!" (44) It was also revealed that contingent "sit down" commands actually increase the frequency of *standing* behavior among students.

Ms. Pedagogue not only recognized that she had been performing this behavior, but that also on occasion it had degenerated into a "shouting match" with students, creating a stressful situation. Inwardly she had been dissatisfied with herself for performing this behavior but had neglected to do anything about it. Upon learning that this form of behavior could make a bad situation worse, she felt a desperate need to try to correct it. She had identified an inappropriate behavior, and thus, theoretically, she was ready for the next step in self-modification of behavior, that of *counting* behaviors.

Counting Behaviors

The second step in self modification of behavior is concerned with actually *counting* how often a target behavior occurs. This means that one obtains a frequency count of the behavior to be improved. If this step is not taken it is difficult to learn the extent to which the behavior is being performed. Sometimes simply counting a behavior will tend to improve it because the teacher is becoming involved in a self-awareness of the behavior. This is to say that counting a behavior calls one's attention to it and how often it is occurring.

In addition to determining the frequency of a behavior, another aspect of this step is what is sometimes called the *ABC Factor* in the behavior modification approach. That is, Antecedent of the behavior, the *Behavior* itself, and the Consequence of the behavior. *Antecedent* is concerned with any event that preceded the behavior and *consequence* is what happens as a result of the behavior. Following are some examples of "ABC's of behavior."

Antecedent	Teacher's Behavior	Consequence
Item 1. Student gets out of his seat.	Teacher shouts at student to "Sit down!"	Class laughs at the teacher.
Item 2. Student talks out to another student.	Teacher shouts at student to "Be quiet!"	Student gives teacher a bored look.
Item 3. Student falls asleep.	Teacher claps hands close to student's ears and awakens him.	Disruption of class by guffaws of other students.

Obviously, it is most important that a teacher develop an awareness of antecedents and consequences of his or her behaviors. The main reason for this is that an antecedent gets a behavior started and a given behavior can result in a unsatisfactory consequence, as in the above illustrations.

Attempting to analyze an antecedent becomes important in terms of a behavior manifested by a teacher. That is, why did the antecedent occur in the first place? In the case of the above examples, questions such as the following might be raised:

Item 1. Why did the student leave his seat? Was he justified in doing so? Did the teacher react too quickly?

Item 2. Why did a student talk out to another student? Was this a persistent behavior of this particular student?

Item 3. Why did the student fall asleep? Was he ill? Has he been doing this before or was it the first time?

The information derived from step two in self modification of behavior is usually designated as *baseline data*. If the information is valid and the behavior frequency is accurate, the teacher then has a *base* from which to operate. This means that the teacher should be in a position to see if attempts at improving a given behavior (step three, *changing behavior*) are meeting with satisfactory results.

Changing Behavior

Any effort to change behavior which has been identified, described, counted, and recorded is referred to as a *plan of intervention*. That is, the teacher intervenes with one or more procedures designed to modify the inappropriate behavior. Any plan to replace an inappropriate behavior with an appropriate one ordinarily involves some sort of *reinforcement* procedure. It has been suggested that, generally speaking, *self*-reinforcement is concerned with changing behavior through self-produced consequences, and further, that these consequences may be overt or covert. Examples are statements to oneself or the acquisition of an item as a reward for one's efforts.

To help in the clarification of Step C in self-modification of behavior, let us return to the hypothetical case of Ms. Pedagogue. It will be recalled that she was dissatisfied with her constant criticism of, and shouting at, some of her sixth graders. She had gone through steps one and two by identifying a target behavior and gathering information in the way of frequency of occurrence, along with an analysis of antecedents and consequences.

In her course in the "Psychology of Teaching" one of the

topics for discussion was "teacher praise versus teacher criticism" in dealing with students. Recognizing that her behavior with her sixth grade class was predominantly characterized by criticism, she took as her term project a study of these two factors—teacher praise and teacher criticism. Her investigation into the literature on the subject revealed the following information:

1. Teacher behavior in such forms as smiles, praise, and words of encouragement, if made contingent upon an appropriate student behavior, tends to increase the frequency of that behavior; therefore, these forms of teacher behavior operate as reinforcers for many student behaviors. (This suggested to Ms. Pedagogue that she might consider minimizing criticism of inappropriate student behavior and maximizing praise for appropriate behavior).

2. Teacher behavior which ignores inappropriate student behavior can be effective in diminishing that behavior. This of course depends upon how disruptive and/or dangerous the behavior might be. Obviously, some types of student behavior cannot be ignored. (This suggested to Ms. Pedagogue that the time she was using to criticize one student for inappropriate behavior might be well spent praising another for appropriate behavior).

3. Teacher behavior in the form of criticism should not be neglected entirely, but rather there should be a ratio between praise *and* criticism, with the former predominating by about five times over the latter. It has been demonstrated that such a ratio can achieve success. Moreover, it has been shown that when things are going poorly in the classroom, teachers criticize students about four or five times more than they praise them (Ms. Pedagogue's behavior had been almost entirely one of criticism).

4. When a teacher criticizes a student it can be done quietly. Conversely, when praise is given it can be done so

with emphasis. Thus, a general principle might be, "Maximize the tone of praise and minimize the tone of criticism." The importance of this has been borne out in studies that show that a loud tone of criticism may likely cause more inappropriate behavior of some students while soft tones may contribute to better control situations for students. (Ms. Pedagogue remembered that in most all instances she had resorted to shouting at students).

5. It may be a good practice for a teacher to criticize an inappropriate behavior without heaping too much criticism on a student. For example, a teacher could emphasize the fact that the student is a "good person," but that the behavior was not so good. Or, from a negative point, "You are not a bad person, but what you did was not good behavior."

With the above information to use as a general guideline, Ms. Pedagogue was ready to set about formulating a plan of intervention. The major objective was to make an effort to reduce or eliminate the inappropriate behavior of criticism accompanied by shouting, and replace it with a more appropriate behavior.

Ms. Pedagogue's task was to intervene with activities that would have some influence on the above situation, and in addition to provide for self-reinforcement when such behaviors were performed. Following are some of the items used in the intervention plan:

1. An effort was made to use less criticism, based upon the undesirability of a given student behavior.

2. An effort was made to use praise for appropriate behavior, not only of a verbal nature but also in the form of smiling, nods of approval and the like.

3. A new voluntary seating plan was devised for the purpose of separating those students who tended to talk out to each other.

4. Cooperative assistance of some of the students was enlisted. This took the form of notifying Ms. Pedagogue when she tended to perform an inappropriate behavior.

This action on the part of Ms. Pedagogue indicated to her students that she was "human" after all.

The next point of concern was that of self-reinforcement. It should be recalled that self-reinforcement is concerned with overt or covert consequences, whether these are statements to oneself or items acquired as a reward for one's efforts. Ms. Pedagogue decided that the major form of self-reinforcement would involve self-praise, or what may sometimes be referred to as "stroking." That is, there is a human need to be applauded for a successful effort, if not by someone else, then by one's self.

In our hypothetical situation, a plan was introduced by Ms. Pedagogue whereby when any member of the class did well in something he literally gave himself a pat on the back. This also included Ms. Pedagogue and it became a common practice for her as well as class members to applaud themselves for a job well done. As far as overt consequences were concerned, on occasion Ms. Pedagogue treated herself to certain luxuries that she had previously been denying herself, such as dining out or purchasing a pair of exotic earrings. (*Note:* The reader is cautioned to remember that the above discussion is hypothetical, perhaps even to the extent that certain aspects of it border on "theoretical extremity" for the purpose of clarifying some points).

Evaluating the Plan of Intervention

The final step in self modification of behavior is concerned with how well the plan of intervention is succeeding; that is, the extent to which the changes in behavior are achieving desired results. This process requires the development of a valid set of evaluative criteria. These criteria can be broad in scope, and thus apply to any problem of self modification of behavior, or they can be more specific and applicable to a particular case. Some examples of general criteria might include:

1. In general, was there an increase in appropriate behavior and/or a decrease in inappropriate behavior?

2. What were the behaviors that achieved the most satisfactory results?

3. What forms of reinforcement appeared to be most successful?

These general evaluative criteria could be applied more specifically in our hypothetical case as follows:

1. Did the teacher notice fewer instances of criticism and shouting on her part by actually keeping an account of this type of behavior? If so, how many?

2. Did the voluntary change in seating plan have any influence on the students who had been "talking out?" If so, in how many instances?

3. Did the system of "patting ourselves on the back" help as a reinforcer in behavior change? If so, in how many ways?

Whatever way one decides to evaluate the plan of intervention, there is still another decision to be made. This also concerns the extent to which the plan has achieved success. If it has met with complete and unequivocal success, it can then perhaps be terminated. Or, if it succeeds only when the behavior change is still being practiced, there may be a need to maintain the procedures. Perhaps the ultimate goal should be to modify behavior to the extent that the problem would be completely eliminated.

CHAPTER 6

HOW TEACHERS CAN DESENSITIZE THEMSELVES TO STRESS

A form of behavior modification known as systematic desensitization is described by one source as "the process of systematically lessening a specific learned fear in an individual." (80) It is purported to provide one means of controlling anxiety. Credit for the development of the technique as a clinical procedure is ordinarily given to Dr. Joseph Wolpe, a psychiatrist, who is said to have introduced it for the purpose of reducing anxiety reactions. (86)

Viewed as a clinical psychotherapeutic procedure, Wolpe's desensitization method consists of repeatedly presenting to the imagination of the deeply relaxed person the feeblest item in a list of anxiety-evoking stimuli, until no more anxiety is evoked. The next item of the list is then presented, and so on, until eventually even the strongest of the anxiety-evoking stimuli fails to evoke any stir of anxiety in the person. Wolpe's process of systematic desensitization involves three phases as follows: (a) training the subject in deep muscle relaxation, (b) constructing an anxiety-evoking hierarchy of stimuli, and (3) counterposing relaxation and the anxiety-evoking stimuli.

Systematic desensitization has been used with success in education, particularly in terms of lessening certain anxieties among students. An example of such an experiment is one in which a 6½-year-old boy was unsuccessful in classroom verbalization. (41) Medical and psychiatric reports did not show any reason for his unwillingness to talk in the classroom. Although the child's test results revealed that he had ability above average, his school progress failed to reach his level of potential. A six-week desensitization program of two sessions per week was developed to try to reduce or eliminate his fear of verbalizing in class. The following hierarchy of anxiety-evoking stimuli was used in the experiment:

1. reading alone to investigator
2. reading alone to roommate
3. reading to two classroom aides
4. reading to teacher and classroom aides
5. reading to teacher, classroom aides, and small group of class peers
6. reading to entire class
7. asking questions or making comments at weekly meetings when all patients, teachers, and staff were present

This program of desensitization met with success in alleviating the child's fear of verbalization in the classroom. Other programs of this same general nature have been used to advantage in reducing test-taking anxiety in students, and in helping to conquer the phobia of school attendance. In this particular connection some child clinical psychologists have found that many school children who are not reading and writing as well as they should are just too frightened to do any better. Otherwise "normal" students have phobias of the disciplines, as other people irrationally fear heights or the sight of blood or dogs. (80)

Many of the phobias connected with reading and writing result from conditioned reactions. After a time the original problem may be resolved, but the barrier to learning which was removed has been replaced by another one, the phobia. Since the child could not read or write well, he or she was probably pretty much a failure in school. The student associates reading and writing with failure and most of them are afraid of failing. In time the fear can grow and the child really needs help. This help almost always comes by *systematically desensitizing* the fear. The approach has been shown to work repeatedly in research laboratories and in practice.

In regard to experiments that concern teachers themselves, it has been suggested that systematically desensitizing teachers to common classroom disruptions may establish competence in self-controlling internal anxious

responses and also provide a solid basis for effectively ignoring student behavior. Some studies have shown some
success in using desensitization to reduce teacher anxiety.
However, little is known about the effects of this procedure on observable teacher and student behavior. Dr. Irving R. Dickman has reported on a systematic desensitization program which was undertaken with teachers in
ghetto schools to help them "react more calmly in their relationships with children; to enable them to cope more adequately and with greater ease with disturbance that occurred in the classroom; and to eliminate the tensions and
frustrations that all too often caused them to overreact frequently with disastrous results." After six sessions, all of
the participating teachers indicated they were more relaxed; and more than half reported that "when they re-
mained calm, the children seemed less fidgety." (19) All
reported a better relationship with the children.

SELF SYSTEMATIC DESENSITIZATION
FOR TEACHERS

Up to this point our discussion has focused primarily
upon systematic desensitization which involves teacher-
student, counselor-client, or therapist-patient relationships. The purpose of this has been to familiarize the reader with the procedure and what it entails. We now turn our
attention to the process of *self*-desensitization with a consideration of its possible use for individual teachers.

Although the value of self-desensitization as a means of
lessening stress-provoking situations has not been completely established by behavioral scientists, some of the research findings are encouraging. For example, one study
reported that self-desensitization was used successfully to
overcome severe public-speaking anxiety. (51)

It has been suggested that systematic self-desensitization is a most interesting and promising procedure

and that such efforts are not likely to be harmful even if they fail. However, self-desensitization should be approached as an experimental procedure. It should be discontinued if the course of anxiety reduction is not relatively smooth, and should be broken off immediately if an increase in anxiety is noted. (84)

An impressive model of systematic self-desensitization, which seems to have particular applicability for teachers, is one suggested by Dr. C. Eugene Walker, Chief of Pediatric Psychology at the University of Oklahoma Medical School, who, incidentally contributed a chapter on the subject to *Stress in Childhood,* the first book in this series.

He introduces the subject of systematic desensitization by stating that many of the anxieties people experience are due to what are termed *conditioned reactions.* These conditioned reactions are identified as stimuli that occur together in our experience and become associated with each other so that we respond to them in the same way, or in a highly similar way, when they occur again. This is to say that if we are made anxious or afraid in the presence of certain stimuli, these same stimuli will make us anxious later when they occur, even if the situation in reality no longer poses an actual threat. Dr. Walker gives as an example a person who may have had a number of experiences as a child, in which a person in authority, such as a school principal, policeman, or guard frightened him and perhaps punished his in some way. As an adult, such a person's reactions to one in authority may cause him considerably more anxiety than the situation really justifies. This is because of his previous conditioning of strong anxiety to an authority figure.

Dr. Walker goes on to suggest that many of our emotions seem to be based on such conditioned reactions. And, that these reactions are somewhat similar to reflexes, but that they are learned rather than inherited. Their automatic or "reflexive" character, however, explains why it is difficult to discuss things rationally with someone who is emotionally involved in a situation. He is responding more with his conditioned reactions to the present stimuli than relating to the actual realities of the situation. (The reader may wish to refer back to the discussion in Chapter 1 regarding learned and unlearned tensions).

The recommendation that Dr. Walker makes for overcoming anxieties in the form of conditioned reactions is the use of systematic self-desensitization, and he presents a highly persuasive case for its effectiveness—provided it is done properly.

In this approach, after a particular problem has been identified, the process consists of three sequential steps: (a) developing a hierarchy of anxiety-evoking stimuli, (b) complete relaxation, and (c) desensitization sessions. Using the previously-mentioned authority figure example, let us apply this to a teacher who has this difficulty where relationship with a school principal is concerned. Incidentally, our surveys show that it is not uncommon for some teachers to have what they designate as a "fear of the principal," without being able to identify reasons for it.

The first step is to take several index cards, writing a different situation or experience on each card that makes for anxiety concerning the problem. The cards are then stacked in order, with the one causing the least anxiety on the top and the one causing the greatest anxiety at the bottom. This is the hierarchy of anxiety-evoking stimuli and might resemble the following:

1. Entering school parking lot and seeing principal's car.

2. Greeting co-workers and discussing principal.

3. Greeting co-worker and co-worker mentions his or her coming meeting with principal.

4. Conferring with co-workers on a meeting time with the principal and co-workers.

5. Walking by principal's office when door is closed.

6. Walking by principal's office when door is open, (no verbalization or eye contact).

7. Walking by principal's office or meeting principal in hall and greeting principal.

8. Arranging meeting with principal.

9. Pre-arranged meeting with principal with many present, such as committee meeting.

10. Pre-arranged meeting with principal with few present, such as a committee meeting.

11. Pre-arranged meeting with principal with only self and principal present.

12. Unscheduled meeting with principal with only self and principal present.

Another possible stress inducing situation could be one in which a given student's behavior produces stress for the teacher. A hierarchy that the teacher might use for self desensitization could be as follows:

1. Anticipating student's presence in school before school begins.

2. Knowledge that student is present in school and will be in class.

3. Anticipating behavior problem during day with the student.

4. Greeting student at the door in the morning.

5. Minor behavior problem arises and is resolved.

6. Minor behavior problem arises and is not resolved.

7. Major behavior problem arises and is resolved.

8. Major behavior problem arises and is not resolved.

9. Verbal or physical confrontation with student in front of class.

Of course the reader must understand that the above hierarchies of anxiety-evoking stimuli are general in nature and each individual would make out his or her own list in more specific detail.

The second step is to try to develop a condition of complete relaxation. (*Note:* The question of how to achieve a relaxed state will be discussed in detail in a portion of the final chapter.) After the person is completely relaxed, the next step in this approach is to begin systematic desensitization. This is done as follows: Look at the top card on the pile, the one that is least anxiety provoking. With eyes closed, and using the imagination, visualize as vividly as possible the situation described on it. That is, imagine the situation occurring, and that one is actually there. If some anxiety is experienced at this point, the imaginary scene should cease immediately and the person should go back to relaxing. After complete relaxation is again obtained, the person is ready to go on. The procedure is continued ✓ until the scene can be imagined without anxiety. Whether this takes only one or two tries, or 15 to 20, it should be repeated until no anxiety is felt. The entire procedure is continued until one has gone through all the cards.

The recommendation is that one work on the scenes in this manner for approximately one half hour at a time. It can be done daily, every other day, or a couple of times a week, depending upon the amount of time one is willing or able to spend, and how quickly one wants to conquer the anxiety. It appears to be a good practice to overlap one or two items from one session to another; that is, beginning a session by repeating an item or two from the previous session which were imagined without anxiety.

One variation of the above procedure is to tape record a description of each scene in advance. One then relaxes and listens to the tape. If anxiety appears, the recorder is turned off and the person goes back to relaxing. When relaxation is again accomplished the individual proceeds as before. A value of using the tape recorder is that there is likely to be better pronunciation, enunciation, and intonation of words. In addition, it may be easier for the individual to concentrate, since he has provided his own auditory input on tape and does not have the additional task of verbalizing and trying to concentrate on the scene at the same time. If desired, the sequence of relaxation procedures can be taped, as well.

✓ After desensitization has been achieved, one can review in one's own mind the preferred action to be taken in the situation that originally caused anxiety. Plans can then be made to do the right thing the next time the situation occurs.

Obviously, the success one experiences with this procedure will depend largely upon the extent to which one is willing to make the painstaking effort involved in the approach. Many persons who have tried it have been so delighted with its effects that they have deliberately sought out situations which previously had caused them great anxiety, frustration, and failure. This is certainly a true test of the value of approach.

CHAPTER 7

INDUCING THE RELAXATION RESPONSE
TO COPE WITH TEACHER STRESS

Most of us need some type of relaxation in order to relieve
the tensions encountered in daily living. The purpose of
this final chapter is to explore various facets of relaxation,
along with those kinds of conditions that tend to produce a
relaxed state. There are many procedures that can improve upon the ability to relax, and it should be borne in
mind that what may be satisfactory for one person may be
unsatisfactory for another.

The reality of muscle fibers is that they have a response
repertoire of one item. All they can do is contract, and this
is the response they make to the electrochemical stimulation of impulses carried via the motor nerves. Relaxation is
the removal of this stimulation.(11)

A relatively new term, *relaxation response,* has been
coined by Dr. Herbert Benson. This involves a number of
bodily changes that occur in the organism when one experiences deep muscle relaxation. There is a response against
"overstress" which brings on these bodily changes and
brings the body back to a healthier balance. (4) Thus, the
purpose of any kind of relaxation technique would be to induce a relaxation response.

From the point of view of the physiologist, relaxation is
sometimes considered a "zero activity," or as nearly zero
as one can manage in the neuromuscular system. That is, it
is a neuromuscular accomplishment that results in a reduction or possibly a complete absence of muscle tone in a
part of, or in the entire body. It has been suggested that a
primary value of relaxation lies in the lowering of brain
and spinal cord activity resulting from a reduction of nerve
impulses that arise in muscle spindles and other sense end-
ings in muscles, tendons and joint structures. (75)

For many years recommendations have been made with

103

regard to procedures that can be applied to achieve relaxation. Examples of some of these procedures are submitted in the ensuing discussions. In consideration of any technique that is designed to accomplish relaxation, it is very important to realize that learning to relax is a skill. This skill is based on the kinesthetic awareness of feeling of *tonus* (the normal degree of contraction present in most muscles which keeps them always ready to function when needed). Unfortunately, it is a skill that very few people use and practice—probably because there is little awareness of how to go about it.

One of the first steps in learning to relax is to experience tension. That is, one should be sensitive to tensions that exist in one's body. This can be accomplished by voluntarily contracting a given muscle group, first very strongly and then less and less. Emphasis should be placed on detecting the signal of tension as the first step in "letting go" (relaxing).

As in the case of any muscular skill, learning how to relax takes time, and one should not expect to achieve complete satisfaction immediately. After one has identified a relaxation technique that he or she feels comfortable with, increased practice should eventually achieve satisfactory results.

In the following sections of this chapter we will take into account the relaxation techniques of *progressive relaxation, meditation,* and *biofeedback.* It seems important at this point to give some attention to the theory underlying these techniques, all of which are concerned with mind-body interactions, and all of which are designed to induce the relaxation response.

In progressive relaxation it is theorized that if the muscles of the body are relaxed, the mind in turn will quiet. The theory involved in meditation is that if the mind is quieted, then other systems of the body will tend to be more readily stabilized. In the practice of biofeedback the theoretical basis tends to involve some sort of integration of progressive relaxation and meditation. It is believed that the brain has the potential for voluntary control over all the systems it monitors, and that is affected by all of these systems. Thus, it is the intimacy of interaction between mind and body that has provided the mechanism through which one can learn voluntary control over biological activity.

The subsequent sections of the chapter will be devoted to discussions of these relaxation techniques, the purpose being to introduce the reader to certain aspects concerned with the techniques.

PROGRESSIVE RELAXATION

The technique of progressive relaxation was developed by Dr. Edmund Jacobson over half a century ago. It is still the technique most often referred to in the literature and probably the one that has had the most widespread application. (Yet, our studies have revealed that only one percent of the teachers surveyed used this technique.) In this technique the person concentrates on progressively relaxing one muscle group after another. The technique is based on the procedure of comparing the difference between tension and relaxation. That is, as previously mentioned, one senses the feeling of tension in order to get the feeling of relaxation.

You might wish to try the traditional experiment used to demonstrate this phenomenon. Raise one arm so that the palm of the hand is facing outward away from your face. Now, bend the wrist backward and try to point the fingers back toward your face and down toward the forearm. You should feel some *strain* at the wrist joint. You should also feel something else in the muscle and this is tension, which is due to the muscle contracting the hand backward. Now, flop the hand forward with the fingers pointing downward and you will have accomplished a *tension-relaxation* cycle.

We have already said that learning to relax is a skill that you can develop in applying the principles of progressive relaxation. One of the first steps is to be able to identify the various muscle groups and how to tense them so that tension and relaxation can be experienced. However, before we make suggestions on how to tense and relax the various muscles, there are certain other preliminary measures that need to be taken into account.

1. You must understand that this procedure takes time, and like anything else, the more you practice the more proficient you would become with the skill.

2. Progressive relaxation is not the kind of thing to be done spontaneously, so you should be prepared to spend from 20 to 30 minutes daily in tensing-relaxing activities.

3. The particular time of day is important, though this is pretty much an individual matter. Some recommendations suggest that progressive relaxation be practiced daily, some time during the day and again in the evening before retiring. For teachers this would be difficult unless one time period was set aside before leaving for school in the morning. This is a good possibility and might help a teacher to start the school day relaxed.

4. It is important to find a suitable place to practice the tensing-relaxing activities. Again, this is an individual matter with some preferring a bed or couch and others a comfortable chair.

5. Consideration should be given to the amount of time a given muscle is tensed. You should be sure that you are able to feel the difference between tension and relaxation.

6. Breathing is an important concomitant in tensing and relaxing muscles. To begin with it is suggested that three or more deep breaths be taken and held for about five seconds. This will tend to make for better rhythm in breathing.

How to Tense and Relax Various Muscles

Muscle groups may be identified in different ways. The classification given here consists of four different groups: (a) muscles of the head, face, tongue, and neck, (b) muscles of the trunk, (c) muscles of the upper extremities, and (d) muscles of the lower extremities.

Muscles of the Head, Face, Tongue and Neck. There are two chief muscles of the head, the one covering the back of the head and one covering the front of the skull. There are about 30 muscles of the face including muscles of the orbit and eyelids, mastication, lips, tongue and neck. Incidentally, it has been pointed out that it takes 26 muscles to frown and a much smaller number to smile. Muscles of this group may be tensed and relaxed as follows: (relaxation is accomplished by "letting go" after tensing)

1. Raise your eyebrows by opening the eyes as wide as possible. You might wish to look into a mirror to see if you have formed wrinkles on the forehead.

2. Tense the muscles on either side of your nose as if you were going to sneeze.

3. Dilate or flare out the nostrils.

4. Force an extended smile from "ear to ear" at the same time clenching your teeth.

5. Pull one corner of the mouth up and then the other up and out as in a "villainous sneer."

6. Draw your chin as close to your chest as possible.

7. Do the opposite of the above trying to draw your head back as close to your back as possible.

Muscles of the Trunk. Included in this group are the muscles of the back, chest, abdomen, and pelvis. Here are some ways you can tense these muscles.

1. Bring your chest forward and at the same time put your shoulders back with emphasis on bringing your shoulder blades as close together as possible.

2. Try to round your shoulders and bring your shoulder

blades far apart. This is pretty much the opposite of the above.

3. Give your shoulders a shrug trying to bring them up to your ears at the same time as you try to bring your neck downward.

4. Breathe deeply and hold it momentarily and then blow out the air from your lungs rapidly.

5. Draw in your stomach so that your chest is out beyond your stomach. Bulge your stomach out so as to make yourself look fatter in that area than you are.

Muscles of the Upper Extremities. This group includes muscles of the hands, forearms, upper arms, and shoulders. A number of muscles situated in the trunk may be grouped with the muscles of the upper extremities, their function being to attach the upper limbs to the trunk and move the shoulders and arms. In view of this there is some overlapping in muscle groups *two* and *three.* Following are some ways to tense some of these muscles:

1. Tense each fist, one at a time as in the isometric activity, the "fist clencher" described in a previous chapter.

2. Raise one arm shoulder high and parallel to the floor. Bend at the elbow and bring the hand in toward the shoulder. Try to touch your shoulder while attempting to move the shoulder away from the hand. Flex your opposite biceps in the same manner.

3. Stretch one arm to the side of the body and try to point the fingers backward toward the body. Do the same with the other arm.

4. Hold the arm out the same way as above, but this time have the palm facing up and point the fingers inward toward the body. Do the same with the other arm.

5. Stretch one arm out to the side, clench the fist and roll the wrist around slowly. Do the same with the other arm.

Muscles of the Lower Extremities. This group includes muscles of the hips, thighs, legs, feet, and buttocks. Following are ways to tense some of these muscles.

1. Hold one leg out straight and point your toes as far forward as you can. Do the same with the other leg.
2. Do the same as the above but point your toes as far backward as you can.
3. Turn each foot outward as far as you can and release. Do just the opposite by turning the foot inward as far as you can.
4. Try to draw the thigh muscles up so that you can see the form of the muscles.
5. Make your buttocks tense by pushing down if you are sitting in a chair. If you are lying down try to draw the muscles of the buttocks in close by attempting to force the cheeks together.

The above suggestions include several possibilities for tensing various muscles of the body. As you practice some of these you will also discover other ways to tense and then let go. A word of caution, though: in the early stages you should be alert to the possibility of cramping certain muscles. This can happen particularly with those muscles that are not frequently used. This means that at the beginning you should proceed carefully. It might be a good idea to keep a record or diary of your sessions so that you can refer back to these experiences if this should be necessary. This will also help you get into each new session by reviewing your experiences in previous sessions.

MEDITATION

It should be mentioned at the outset that a tremendous amount of literature has been published on the subject of meditation in recent years. Thus, the comments devoted to meditation here present only a general overview of the subject, along with suggestions as to how one might consider proceeding with this particular relaxation technique.

The Eastern art of meditation dates back more than 2,000 years. Until recently, this ancient art has been associated with particular religious as well as cultural connotations. In the 1960s, countercultures began using it as a route to a more natural means of living and relaxing. Today, people from all walks of life can be counted among the untold numbers of those around the world who practice and realize the positive effects that meditation has upon the human mind and body.

Meditation has been described as a mental exercise which requires an individual to attend mentally or concentrate on a certain subject. Although there are many meditation techniques, *concentration* is the essential factor contributing to success. The mind's natural flow from one idea to another is quieted by the individual's concentration. Lowering mental activity may seem an easy task, but almost total elimination of scattered thought takes a great deal of time and practice on the part of the meditator.

The previously mentioned Dr. Herbert Benson finds that meditation decreases the body's metabolic rate, with the following decreases in body function involved: (a) oxygen consumption, (b) breathing rate, (c) heart rate and blood pressure, (d) sympathetic nervous system activity, and (e) blood lactate (a chemical produced in the body during stress).

Only recently has the scientific community recognized the positive effects that the repeated practice of meditation has upon those who are stress-ridden. Various scientific studies have shown that meditation can actually decrease the possibility that an individual will contract stress-related disorders, and that meditators have a much faster recovery rate when exposed to stressful situations than non-meditators. In addition, meditation is said to increase the psychological stability of those who practice it as well as to reduce anxiety. Such research seems to be disclosing that meditation can be a path to better health.

The question is sometimes raised whether sleep and

meditation are the same thing. Sleep can be likened to meditation in that both are hypometabolic states; that is, restful states in which the body experiences decreased metabolism. But meditation is not a form of sleep. Dr. Benson indicates that oxygen consumption as well as alpha brain activity are different in sleep states. Although some similar psychological changes have been found in sleep and meditation, the two are not the same and one is not a substitute for the other. In this regard, it is interesting to note, various studies have shown that meditation may restore more energy than sleep.

Although there are many meditation techniques, research tends to show that one technique is about as good as another for improving the way stress is handled. (32) Regardless of the technique used there are certain basic considerations which might well be taken into account. The following descriptive list of these basic considerations is general in nature, and the reader can make his or her own specific application as best fits individual needs and interests.

Locate a Quiet Place and Assume a Comfortable Position.   The importance of a quiet environment should be obvious since concentration is facilitated in a tranquil surrounding. The question of the position one may assume for meditation is an individual matter. However, when it is suggested that one assume a comfortable position, this might be amended by, "but not too comfortable." The reason for this is that if one is too comfortable there is always the possibility of falling asleep, and this of course would defeat the purpose of meditation. This is a reason why one should not take a lying position while meditating. A position might be taken where there is some latitude for "swaying." This can provide for a comfortable posture and at the same time possibly guard against the individual "falling into dreamland." The main consideration is that the person be in a comfortable enough position to remain this way for a period of 20 minutes or so. One such position would be to sit on the floor with crossed legs, straight back, and resting on the legs and buttocks. Your head should be erect and the hands resting in the lap. If you prefer to sit in a chair rather than on the floor, select a chair with a straight back. You need to be the judge of comfort and thus you should select a position where you feel you are able to concentrate and remain in this position for a period of time.

Focus Your Concentration. As mentioned before, concentration is the essential key to successful meditation. If you focus on one specific thing such as an object or a sound or a personal feeling it is less likely that your thoughts will be distracted. One source suggests that the meditator might consider focusing on such things as a fantasy trip, re-experiencing a trip already taken, a place that has not been visited, a poem, a certain sound, or a chant. (80)

Use of a Nonsense Word or Phrase. Some techniques of meditation such as the popular Transcendental Meditation (TM), involve the chanting of a particular word (mantra) as one meditates. Although the mantra has important meaning for the meditator, we refer to it as a nonsense word because it should be devoid of any connotation which would send one thinking in many directions. This, of course, would hinder concentration. Because of this a nonsense word would perhaps be most effective. Incidentally, we have found that in our own personal experience with meditation, the practice of chanting such a word is very effective.

Be Aware of a Natural Breathing Rhythm. The importance of a natural breathing rhythm should not be underestimated. In fact, some clinical psychologists recommend this as a means of concentration. That is, one can count the number of times he or she inhales and exhales, and this in itself is a relaxing mental activity

The Time for Meditation. Because meditation is an activity to quiet the mind we strongly recommend that the practice not be undertaken immediately upon arriving home from school. At this time the mind may be in a very active state of reviewing the day's activities. Our own personal experience suggests a 20-minute period in the morning before school, and a 20-minute period in the evening preferably before dinner, or possibly two hours after dinner.

The following is a description of a procedure that the authors have personally found successful. Again, however, it should be mentioned that it is pretty much an individual matter and what works for one person may not work as well for another.

To begin with, assume a comfortable position in a quiet place with as passive an attitude as possible. Try to dismiss all wandering thoughts from your mind and concentrate on a relaxed body while keeping the eyes closed. When feeling fairly relaxed the repetition of the nonsense word or phrase can begin. This can be repeated orally or silently. We suggest repeating it silently; that is, in the mind. Repeat your chosen word or phrase in this manner over and over, keeping the mind clear of any passing thoughts. At first this may be very difficult but with practice it becomes easier.

After a period of about 15 or 20 minutes have passed, discontinue repetition of the word or phrase. Become aware of your relaxed body once again. Give yourself a few moments before moving, as your body will need to readjust. For successful prolonged results one might consider continuing this practice two times daily in 20-minute sessions.

If you have difficulty trying to meditate on your own it is possible to seek the services of an experienced meditator for assistance and supervision. The recent widespread popularity of meditation as a relaxation technique has been accompanied by the establishment of meditation centers for instruction in some communities.

In closing this section of the chapter we should reiterate that whether or not one chooses meditation as a relaxation technique is an individual matter. Only two percent of the teachers in our surveys used meditation as a means of coping with stress; however, all of these respondents reported great success with the technique and recommended it for others.

BIOFEEDBACK

In our discussion of biofeedback it should be made luminously clear that we are dealing with a complex and complicated subject. It will be our purpose to discuss this phenomenon in terms of what it is supposed to be and what it is supposed to do. It should be borne in mind that, at least in the early stages of biofeedback training (BFT), it is important that it take place under qualified supervision. This means that should you wish to pursue an interest in, and eventually participate in BFT, you would do well to seek the services of one trained in this area.

The Meaning of Biofeedback

The term *feedback* has been used in various frames of reference. It may have been used originally in engineering in connection with control systems that involve feedback procedures. These feedback control systems make adjustments to environmental changes as in the case of a thermostat controlling temperature levels in the home.

The term feedback has been used interchangeably with the expression *knowledge of results* by learning theorists to describe the process of providing the learner with information as to the accuracy of his reactions; or in other words, feedback is knowledge which the performer receives about his performance. With particular reference to motor-skill learning, some psychologists are of the opinion that feedback in the form of knowledge of results is the strongest, most important variable controlling performance and learning, and further, studies have repeatedly shown that without it there is no improvement; with it, there is progressive improvement and after its withdrawal there is deterioration.

Modern writers on the subject of biofeedback seem to describe it in essentially the same way although some may elaborate more in determining its precise meaning. That is, some merely state what it is while others may extend the description to include what it does. For example, one source describes it as any information that is received about the functioning of our internal organs such as the heart, sweat glands, muscles and brain. (76) Another similar description indicates that it is a process in which information about an organism's biological activity is supplied for perception by the same organism. (10) Another source extends this somewhat by including under the term biofeedback the monitoring of signals from the body such as muscle tension and hand warmth, and the feeding of that information back to individuals through the use of sophisticated machines, in order to provide those individuals with external information as to exactly what is happening in their bodies. (17)

One authority on the subject, Dr. Barbara B. Brown, has estimated that there are perhaps millions of individual feedback systems in the human body. She comments that information about the external environment is sensed by any of the five senses and relayed to a control center, usually the brain, where it is integrated with other relevant information and when the sensed information is significant enough, central control generates commands for appropriate body changes. She cites as examples of feedback control systems, responses of scratching an itch, hitting a baseball with a bat, pupil accommodation for near and far vision, perspiration, sneezing, sleeping, urinating, and eating. (11)

Biofeedback Instrumentation

We are all aware of the fact that the human body itself is a complicated and complex biofeedback instrument which alerts us to certain kinds of internal activity, as mentioned in the previous discussion. However, many students of the

subject feel that there is still a need for sensitive instruments to monitor physiological and psychological reactivity. Following is a brief discussion of some of the more
widely known biofeedback instruments which are used for
both research and therapeutic purposes.

Electromyograph (EMG).   Electromyography is the recording of electrical phenomena occurring in muscles during contraction. Needle or skin electrodes are used and
connected with an oscilloscope so that action potentials
may be viewed and recorded. Before the electromyograph
was available, for the most part guesswork had to be used
to try to determine the participation of muscles in movement. Electromyography helps to determine what muscles, or even parts of muscles participate in movement.
When a muscle is completely relaxed or inactive it has no
electric potential. When it is engaged in contraction, current appears.

It is believed that EMG training can produce deep muscle relaxation and thus relieve tension. A person gets the
feedback by seeing a dial or hearing a sound from the ma-
chine and thus he knows immediately the extent to which
certain muscles may be tensed or relaxed. A muscle frequently used in EMG training for research and other purposes is the *frontalis* located in the forehead.

Another important aspect of EMG training is concerned
with retraining a person following an injury or disease
when there is a need to observe small increments of gain in
function of a muscle.

Feedback Thermometers.   The obvious purpose of feedback thermometers is to record body temperatures. Ordinarily, a thermistor is attached to the hands or the fingers.
This highly sensitive instrument shows very small increments of degrees of temperature change so that the person
receives the information through a visual or auditory signal. This kind of feedback instrumentation has been recommended for such purposes as reduction of stress and
anxiety, and autonomic nervous system relaxation.

Electroencephalograph (EEG). The purpose of this instrument is to record amplitude and frequency of brain waves, and it has been used in research for many years. It has also been used with success to diagnose certain clinical diseases. In addition, feedback EEG has found a use in psychotherapy and in reducing pain as well as stress.

An interesting relatively recent horizon for EEG feedback is how it might be involved in creativity and learning. In fact, some individuals involved in creative activity have indicated that they can emerge from the EEG *theta* state with answers to problems that they previously were unable to solve. The theta waves are ordinarily recorded when a person is in a state of drowsiness or actually falling asleep. It is perhaps for this reason that this condition has been referred to by some as "sleep learning." Since it is a state just before sleep, others refer to it as the twilight period or *twilight learning*.

The previously mentioned Dr. Barbara B. Brown contends that EEG could maximize the usefulness of teaching machines. She suggests that the color of the recording screen could be controlled by two basic brain wave patterns, the "alert" EEG associated with high attention levels, and the "nonalert" EEG pattern associated with inattention. Similarly, physical and mental attitudes more suitable for learning could be acquired more readily, and the attention span could be improved by one's own volition.

Galvanic Skin Response (GSR). There are several different kinds of GSR instruments used to measure changes in electrical resistance of the skin to detect emotional arousal. The instrument reacts in proportion to the amount of perspiration one emits and the person is informed of the change in electrical resistance by an auditory or visual signal. One aspect of GSR is made use of in the polygraph or lie detector, which records a response that is supposed to be associated with lying. GSR feedback is oftentimes recommended for use in relaxation, reducing tension, improvement of ability to sleep, and emotional control.

In general the purpose of biofeedback machinery is to (a) provide accurate and reliable data which will increase one's awareness of how the body is functioning and, (b) demonstrate one's influence on the actions of one's own body. It is hoped that this information should be useful in inspiring a person to take an active interest in his own well-being. After such information is received, if it has been obtained under the supervision of a qualified therapist, a given number of sessions may be arranged for consultation and training. Perhaps the ultimate objective is for the individual to be able to gain control over his own autonomic nervous system.

As popular and well advertised as biofeedback machinery has become, it is not without its critics. One such authority on mind-body relationships is Dr. Beata Jencks, who feels that many of the same goals can be accomplished, without artificial devices, by using the body as its own feedback instrument. In fact, she identifies over a dozen of these, including among others (a) diverse muscle relaxation, (b) change of heart rate and body temperature, (c) change of breathing patterns, (d) decrease of stress and anxiety reactions, (e) mental relaxation, (f) autonomic nervous system relaxation, (g) pain relief for tension headaches, backaches, and other aches and pains and (h) improved learning ability, including enhancement of concentration and recall. She indicates, however, that certain of the biofeedback instruments, particularly the EMG, have important applications in the retraining of patients following injury and disease. (38)

At the present time it is difficult to determine unequivocally what the future of biofeedback might be. Without question it has influenced our way of thinking about how it may be possible for a person to be able to control his physiological functions. In view of this, perhaps one of the foremost contributions of biofeedback is that it creates in an individual a feeling of his own responsibility for personal well-being. It has been suggested that if biofeedback as a research methodology and treatment approach can survive biofeedback as a fad, then it may provide a useful tool which will change our conception of the human body. (76)

All of the techniques discussed in this chapter as well as other recommendations made throughout the book have been employed with varying degrees of success by persons who have practiced them. Individual differences suggest that one teacher may find more success than another with given procedures. One of the most important factors to take into account is that dealing with stress is pretty much an individual matter. With practice most of you will have some degree of success in your attempts to manage your own stressful conditions. Above all, a positive attitude toward life in general is an essential prerequisite for any kind of stress control program that is undertaken.

REFERENCES

1. *Adult Physical Fitness.* Washington, D.C.; U. S. Government Printing Office, 1976.
2. Aptekar, L., "Teacher Resentment and Burnout in High Schools." *High School Journal,* February/March 1984.
3. Auerbach, Stuart, "Doctors Say Studies Fail to Prove That Stress Causes Heart Attacks." *The Washington Post,* January 22, 1975.
4. Benson, Herbert, *The Relaxation Response.* New York, William Morrow, 1975.
5. Bimler, R., "Steps in Developing Stress—And Enjoying it Less." *Lutheran Education,* January/February 1985.
6. Blase, J. J., "Social-Psychological Grounded Theory of Teacher Stress and Burnout." *Educational Administration Quarterly,* Fall 1982.
7. Bloch, Alfred M., "The Battered Teacher." *Today's Education,* March/April 1977.
8. Bradley R. C., "Taking Stress Out of Student Teaching." *Clearing House,* September 1984.
9. Brodsky, Carroll M., "Long-Term Work Stress in Teachers and Prison Guards." *Journal of Occupational Medicine,* February 1977.
10. Brown, Barbara B., *The Biofeedback Syllabus.* Springfield, Il: Thomas 1975.
11. Brown, Barbara B., *Stress and the Art of Biofeedback.* New York: Bantam 1978.
12. Cannon, Walter B., *The Wisdom of the Body.* New York: W. W. Norton, 1932.
13. Cassel, R. N., "Critical Factors Related to Teacher Burnout." *Education,* Fall 1984.
14. Cedoline, Anthony J., *The Effect of Affect.* San Rafael, CA; Academic Therapy Publications, 1977.
15. Coates, Thomas J., and Thoresen, Carl E., "Teacher Anxiety: A Review of Recommendations." *Review of Educational Research,* Spring 1976.
16. Coursey, Robert D., "To Sleep or Not to Sleep—That is the Problem." *Precis,* College Park, MD, September 12, 1977.

121

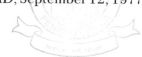

122

17. Culligan, Matthew J., and Sedlacek, Keith, *How to Kill Stress Before It Kills You*. New York: Grosset & Dunlap, 1976.
18. Cunningham, W. G., "Research-Based Strategies for Fighting Teacher Burnout." *Educational Digest*, May 1982.
19. Dickman, Irving R., *Behavior Modification*. New York, Public Affairs Pamphlet No. 540, 1976.
20. *Dictionary of Education*. 2nd ed. Carter V. Good, Ed. New York, McGraw-Hill, 1959.
21. Dunham, J., "Stress in Schools." *Times Education Supplement, July 1982*.
22. Dunham, J., "Disruptive Pupils and Teacher Stress." *Educational Research*, June 1981.
23. Favell, Judith Elbert, *The Power of Positive Reinforcement: A Handbook of Behavior Modification*. Springfield, IL: Thomas, 1977.
24. Feitler, F. C., and Tokar, E., "Getting a Handle on Teacher Stress: How Bad Is the Problem?" *Educational Leadership*, March 1982.
25. Fimian, M. J., "What Is Teacher Stress?" *Clearing House*, November 1982.
26. Forman, S. G., and O'Malley, P. L., "School Stress and Anxiety Interventions." *School Psychological Review*, Spring 1984.
27. Freese, Arthur S., "Understanding Stress." New York, Public Affairs Pamphlet No. 538, 1976.
28. Frey, D. and Young, J. A., "Methods School Administrators Can Use to Help Teachers Manage Stress." *NASSP Bulletin*, March 1983.
29. Friedman, Meyer and Rosenman, Ray H., *Type A Behavior and Your Heart*. New York: Alfred A. Knopf, 1974.
30. Gal, Reuven and Lazarus, Richard S., "The Role of Activity in Anticipating and Confronting Stressful Situations." *Journal of Human Stress*, December 1975.
31. Gold, Y., "Burnout: A Major Problem for the Teaching Profession." *Education*, Spring 1984.
32. Goleman, Daniel, "Meditation Helps Break the Stress Spiral." *Psychology Today*, February 1976.
33. Hicks, F. P., *The Mental Health of Teachers*. New York: Cullman Ghertner, 1933.
34. Humphrey, James H. and Humphrey, Joy N., "Factors

123

Which Induce Stress in Teachers." *Stress, The Official Journal of the International Institute of Stress,* Winter 1981.
34. Humphrey, James H., and Humphrey, Joy N., *Child Learning.* 2nd ed., Dubuque, IA: Wm. C. Brown, 1974.
35. Humphrey, Joy N., and Everly, George S., "Perceived Dimensions of Stress Responsiveness in Male and Female Students." *Health Education,* November/December, 1980.
36. Humphrey, Joy N., and Humphrey, James H., "Incidents in the School Environment Which Induce Stress in Upper Elementary School Children." College Park, MD, 1977.
37. "Instructor Survey Reveals Stress, Weight Control, Top Concerns of Teachers Nationwide." *Instructor,* February 1977.
38. Jencks, Beata, *Your Body Biofeedback at Its Best.* Chicago: Nelson Hall, 1977.
39. Kalker, P. "Teacher Stress and Burnout: Causes and Coping Strategies." *Contemporary Education,* Fall 1984.
40. Knapp, T. J. and Shodahl, S. A., "Ben Franklin as a Behavior Modifier: a Note." *Behavior Therapy,* 5, 1974.
41. Kravetz, R. and Forness, S., "The Special Classroom as a Desensitization Setting." *Exceptional Children,* 37, 1971.
42. Lazarus, Richard S., "The Self-Regulation of Emotion." In L. Levy, Ed. *Parameters of Emotion,* New York, Raven Press, 1975.
43. Liberty, P. G., et al., "Concern with Mastery and Occupational Attraction." *Journal of Personality,* 34, 1966.
44. Madsen, C. H., et al., "An Analysis of the Reinforcing Function of 'Sit Down' Commands." In R. K. Parks, Ed. *Readings in Educational Psychology,* Boston: Allyn & Bacon, 1968.
45. Madsen, C. H., et al., "Rules, Praise and Ignoring: Elements of Elementary Classroom Control." *Journal of Applied Behavior Analysis,* 1, 1968.
46. Maples, Mary F., "Stress: In Defense of Its Positive Dimensions." *The Journal of the Association of Teacher Educators,* Fall 1980.
47. Mason, John W., et al., "Selectivity of Corticosteroids and Catecholamine Responses to Various Natural Stimuli." In George Serban, Ed. *Psychopathology of Human Adaptation,* New York: Plenum Publishing Company, 1976.

124

48. Mattson, K. D., "Personality Traits Associated with Effective Teaching in Rural and Urban Secondary Schools." *Journal of Educational Psychology,* 66, 1974.
49. McQuade, Walter and Aikan, Ann, *Stress.* New York: E. P. Dutton, 1974.
50. Merry, Frieda and Merry Ralph, *The First Two Decades of Life.* New York: Harper and Row, 1958.
51. Migler, B. and Wolpe, Joseph, "Automated Self-Desensitization: A Case Report." *Behavior Research and Therapy,* 5, 1967.
52. Milstein, M. M. and Golaszewski, G., "Effects of Organizationally Based Stress Management Efforts in Elementary School Settings." *Urban Education,* January 1985.
53. Moracco, J. C., and McFadden, H., "Counselor's Role in Reducing Teacher Stress." *Personnel and Guidance Journal,* May 1982.
54. Morehouse, Laurence E. and Gross, Leonard, *Total Fitness in Thirty Minutes a Week.* New York: Simon and Schuster, 1977.
55. Morehouse, Laurence E. and Gross Leonard, *Maximum Performance.* New York: Simon and Schuster, 1977.
56. National Education Association, Department of Classroom Teachers, *Fit to Teach: A Study of Health Problems of Teachers.* Washington, D.C., 1938.
57. National Education Association, "Teaching Load in 1950." *Research Bulletin,* Washington, D.C., 1951.
58. National Education Association, "Teacher Problems," *Research Bulletin,* Washington, D.C., 1967.
59. O'Leary, K. Daniel, et al., "The Effects of Loud and Soft Reprimands on the Behavior of Disruptive Students," *Exceptional Children,* 37, 1970.
60. Palestini, H., "Teacher Peer Counseling Approach to Teacher Stress," *Momentum,* May 1984.
61. Palm, J. Daniel, *Diet Away Your Stress, Tension and Anxiety,* New York: Doubleday, 1976.
62. Parsons, J. S., *Anxiety and Teaching Competence.* Diss., Palo Alto, CA; Stanford University, 1971. *Dissertation Abstracts International.*
63. Payne, R. and Fletcher, B., "Job Demands, Supports, and Constraints as Predictors of Psychological Strain Among

School Teachers," *Journal of Vocational Behavior*, April 1983.
64. Pelletier, Kenneth R., *Mind as Healer Mind as Slayer*, New York; Dell, 1977.
65. Perkins, Hugh, *Human Development and Learning*, 2nd ed. Belmont, CA: Wadsworth, 1974.
66. Posner, Israel and Leitner, Lewis A., "Eustress vs. Distress: Determination of Predictability and Controllability of the Stressor." *Stress, The Official Journal of the International Institute of Stress*, Summer, 1981.
67. Remer, R., "Personal Approaches to Stress Reduction: A Workshop," *School Psychological Review*, Spring 1984.
68. Richards, R. R. and Johnson, R. A., "The Nominal Group Technique as a Way for Teachers to Define Stressors." *Educational Research Quarterly*, No. 2, 1984–85.
69. Seaward, M. R., "Avoiding Burnout—The Personal Development of the Teacher." *Journal of Business Education*, April 1984.
70. Schuessler, Raymond, "The Man Who Revolutionized Our Schools." *NRTA Journal*, September/October 1977.
71. Seyle, Hans, *The Stress of Life*, New York, McGraw-Hill, 1956.
72. Seyle, Hans, *Stress Without Distress*, New York, Signet New American Library, 1975.
73. Smith, D. and Milstein, M. M., "Stress and Teachers: Old Wine in New Bottles." *Urban Education*, April 1984.
74. "Status of the American Public School Teacher," Washington, D.C. *NEA Research*, 1975–76.
75. Steinhaus, Arthur, *Toward an Understanding of Health and Physical Education.* Dubuque, IA; William C. Brown, 1963.
76. Stern, Robert M. and Ray, William J., *Biofeedback and the Control of Internal Bodily Activity.* Homewood, IL: Learning Systems Company, 1975.
77. St. John, J., "A Hands-On (Literally!) Approach to Stress Reduction—What's New in Schools?" *Thrust*, June 1984.
78. Sylwester, Robert, "Stress." *Instructor*, March 1977.
79. Viscott, David, *The Language of Feeling*, New York: Arbor House, 1976.
80. Walker, C. Eugene, *Learn to Relax, 13 Ways to Reduce Tension*, Englewood Cliffs, NJ: Prentice-Hall 1975.

81. Wangberg, E. G., "Helping Teachers Cope with Stress." *Educational Leadership*, March 1982.
82. Wangberg, E. G., "The Complex Issue of Teacher Stress and Job Dissatisfaction." *Contemporary Education*, Fall 1984.
83. Warder, V. G., "Stress Stoppers." *Instructor*, August 1984.
84. Watson, David R. and Tharp, Roland, *Self-Directional Behavior: Self-Modification for Personal Adjustment.* Belmont, CA: Wadsworth, 1972.
85. Wolff, Harold C., *Stress and Disease.* Springfield, IL: Thomas 1968, 2nd ed. revised and edited by Stewart Wolff and Helen Godell, 1968.
86. Wolpe, Joseph, *The Practice of Behavior Therapy.* 2nd ed, New York: Pergamon Press, 1973.
87. "What Does the Public Think of the Schools?" *Today's Education*, November/December, 1977.
88. Zimmerman, B. H., "The Relationship Between Teacher Classroom Behavior and Student School Anxiety Levels," *Psychology in Schools.* July 1970.

INDEX

127